the simple guide to Planted AQUARIUMS

Barber & Wilson

t.f.h.

T.F.H. Publications, Inc.

T.F.H. Publications, Inc.
One TFH Plaza
Third and Union Avenues
Neptune City, NJ 07753

Barber, Terry Ann.
The simple guide to planted aquariums / Terry Ann Barber and Rhonda Wilson.
p. cm.
Includes bibliographical references and index.
ISBN 0-7938-2117-7 (alk. paper)
1. Aquariums. 2. Aquarium fishes. 3. Aquarium plants. I. Wilson, Rhonda. II. Title.
SF457.3.B368 2005
635.9'674--dc22
2004027606

This book has been published with the intent to provide accurate and authoritative information in regard to the subject matter within. While every precaution has been taken in preparation of this book, the author and publisher expressly disclaim responsibility for any errors, omissions, or adverse effects arising from the use or application of the information contained herein. The techniques and suggestions are used at the reader's discretion and are not to be considered a substitute for veterinary care. If you suspect a medical problem, consult your veterinarian.

Dedicated to the care and well-being of companion animals for over 50 years.
www.tfhpublications.com

Contents

Choose Your Style!

Don't forget the Test Kits!

Part One

Plan Before You Plant

"Maybe the maple tree was overkill."

The Joy of Planted Aquariums

Keeping plants in the home aquarium is not new. However, the interest in keeping aquatic plants has blossomed into a complete hobby unto itself. You will hear the term "aquatic gardening," which shows that the emphasis has gone from fish keeping to plant keeping.

A modern, fully planted aquarium is a beautiful thing to behold. The plants make the aquarium look like an underwater forest or jungle. Plants of all sizes and textures are used to create the lush landscape. You will see fish dart in and out of the scene—red, blue, and flashing silver.

You can create this lovely scene in your own

Planted aquariums can make beautiful additions to any home.

Fish and Plants

Part of the art of planted aquarium keeping is matching your animals to the environment. Many fish species are not good candidates for a fully planted tank. Many are ideal but may be predators of other animals that you want to keep. You will need to know about your plants and animals to create your perfect "waterscape." It would be really frustrating to create a salad for a fish or buy that really cool fresh water shrimp and see it get eaten as soon as you put it in the tank.

aquarium. A little knowledge, a little work, and your own special sense of design will help you create a magic water world of your own. This book will give you the basic knowledge that you will need to get started.

History of Planted Tanks

The earliest verifiable evidence of fish keeping dates back to about 2500 B.C. Ancient people such as the Persians, Egyptians, Chinese, Greeks, and Romans kept live fish for food or ornament. There are many ancient mosaics and other works of art depicting fish. The origin of goldfish may have been in Persia, but it was in China more than 1000 years ago that they really started being bred and developed. Goldfish moved to Japan in the early 1600s. Our fascination with aquatics has developed over a great deal of our recorded history.

The real foundation for the modern aquarium was set in the mid 1800s. The Victorians loved nature. They made nature crafts and tried to find ways to bring nature indoors. They also loved plants, particularly ferns and palms. In the 1850s, the real popularity of aquariums was underway. The Wardian cases were lovely ornate terrariums, and the Warrington cases were their lovely aquatic counterparts.

In the late 1700s, Antoine Lavoisier became the first person on record to keep fish in glass bowls and jars.

The aquariums from this time period were incredible works of art. Public aquariums were also popular during this period, and it was during the late 1800s that many great advances and introductions were made to the aquarium hobby. The first aquarium magazine appeared in the United States at this time; it was published by Hugo Mulertt, a pioneer of the hobby. An engraving of the Madagascar Lace Plant was included in a 1916 edition. Near the turn of the century in Germany, Adolph Kiel had 32 greenhouses full of aquatic plants. In Europe, he was known as the "father of aquatic plants."

During this time, the theory of aquarium keeping was the

balanced aquarium. Plants, snails, fish, and other animals were to balance each other out to make true miniature systems. Though popular at the time, this idea has since been refuted. Plants were very important to the Victorian aquarium. Some plants that were available to hobbyists in the late 1800s included *Sagittaria, Ludwigia, Cabomba, Myriophyllum, Riccia, Chara, Salvinia*, and water hyacinth, all of which are still well known and still used today.

Ludwigia has been available to hobbyists since the 1800s!

Early ideas for pumps, heaters, and other equipment really began to flow in the early 1900s. A lot of that equipment would be unrecognizable today. It was during this time that the Dutch aquariums were developing and had become an established style of aquarium by the 1930s. Vintage aquarium equipment also developed at this time. You probably wouldn't recognize the equipment in the early 1900s, but it was starting to look similar to the equipment of today by the mid 1930s.

There were quite a few aquarium books being published in the 1930s. One of these was *Tropical Fishes for a Private Aquarium*, which was written by Christopher W. Coates and published in 1933. It lists quite a few aquarium plants and recommends *Vallisneria, Sagittaria, Elodea*, and *Cabomba*. He also recommended various *Cryptocoryne* species "where strong light is not available." Floating plants mentioned in the book were *Riccia* and Bladderwort. Miscellaneous plants listed were *Salvinia, Azolla*, Duckweed, Hornworts, *Myriophyllum*, and *Ludwigia*.

As to the chemistry of the 1930s aquarium, the book does discuss the exchange of oxygen and carbon dioxide and pH and the negative effects of acidity on fish. The effect of pH in the aquarium was introduced in the late 1920s. Of course, there was no mention of ammonia or nitrogen.

Exotic Tropical Fishes was published in 1938. The book was written by Dr. William T. Innes and is often referred to as "The Innes Book." This was the aquarists' Bible for many years and is still regarded as such by many old-timers.

The aquarium hobby continued to grow. A 1953 book by Ruthven Todd, *The Tropical Fish Book*, shows pages of wonderful streamlined, shiny, metal-framed tanks. Of course, there were also ceramic divers in those large and clunky vintage diving suits.

Equipment has continued to improve, and the metal frames have left. New filters have been developed, as has a better understanding of aquarium chemistry. New and improved foods have been created. New fish and plants have come into the hobby, and hobbyists have learned how to take better care of them.

In recent years, new planted-tank techniques have become available with the use of better lighting and CO_2. A wealth of new plants and animals has become available, giving hobbyists an exciting selection.

A Social Event

Sharing information with like-minded hobbyists is a wonderful aspect to the planted-aquarium hobby. I highly recommend getting connected so that you can bounce ideas off others and get quick help for any problems you may have.

Clubs

You may have a local aquarium club. In that club, there are probably people who are keeping planted aquariums. Freshwater-focused clubs are the first place to look, but many saltwater fish keepers like planted aquariums, as you can approach their creation much like that of a reef tank–and there are saltwater plants too!

National clubs also offer more specific information on planted tanks. Most national clubs have a yearly convention. Attending a national convention is a great way to meet people who are specialists in the hobby. It is also a neat way to meet people from all over the world. Be sure to check out the Resources section at the end of this book for more specific information on clubs.

Online

The Internet is the place to be for fast facts. There are many web sites devoted to planted aquariums. Even better, you can find bulletin boards where people post questions, answers, and ideas on all aspects of planted aquarium keeping. If you aren't on the Internet yet, this is a great reason to try it out.

Play It Safe

Safety is such an important topic that it needs to be right here. I will point out safety issues as we go along, but there are a few that you should think about before you set up your aquarium. Aquarium keeping is a very safe hobby, but there are a few things that you should be aware of to keep you and your family safe. Let's go over these safety items that you need to know.

Electricity and Water Don't Mix

Everybody knows that it is unsafe to mix water and electricity. Water is a very good electrical conductor. When you stand in a puddle, you give the current a direct path to the ground, right through you! There is enough juice in your household current to kill.

There are building codes specific to areas of the home where water and electricity can come into contact. For example, it is now code to have a Ground Fault Interruption Circuit (GFIC) in bathrooms and garages. A GFIC is a simple device that can save your life.

In your household wiring, electricity flows into an appliance and back out again. The GFIC has its own little circuit that measures the current going out and coming back. If there is a failure to ground (in other words, the electricity doesn't come back), it shuts off the circuit. No more current. This means if you have your hands in the tank and break the glass of the heater, you will live to tell about it.

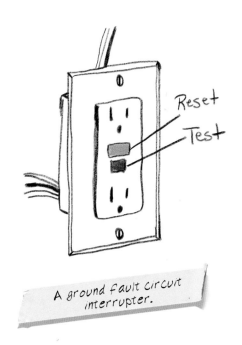

A ground fault circuit interrupter.

GFICs can be purchased in many forms. The least expensive and most readily available is a replacement for your household electrical plug. It has a little red button that is used for testing and as a reset button. It is a very good idea to test the circuit once in a while to make sure it is working. Just push the red button and it should turn off the outlet. A good time to test is just before you plan to work around your aquarium.

GFICs can also be purchased as part of an extension cord. These are a little more expensive but are well worth the cost. Many folks have an extension cord running into the tank cabinet. This is a great place to put your GFIC. Most home improvement stores will carry both types of GFICs.

Gas Cylinder Safety

If you really get into aquatic-plant keeping, you may decide to use bottled carbon dioxide. Using compressed gas also requires some safety precautions. We will discuss these more in detail in the equipment section. Just be aware that gas cylinders require careful handling.

What Type of Planted Tank Suits You?

The planted tank hobby has developed sufficiently that there are several styles and types of tanks that you can create. The design of your tank is where you can use your own sense of style as a way to express yourself and your interests. Let's talk about some of the types and styles of planted aquariums that have evolved. You can take ideas here and there to create something that pleases you. Most people think of aquariums as places to keep fish, but they can become a medium to create your own unique style.

Biotope aquariums are created to mimic a specific aquatic environment, and natural aquariums attempt a natural-like creation with as little technology as possible. These are

Natural aquariums attempt a natural-like creation with little technology.

termed low-tech tanks, as opposed to high-tech tanks, which rely heavily on filtration, CO_2, and conditioners.

The Dutch Aquarium

It's not surprising these lovely tanks developed in Holland, the land of the beautiful Dutch bulbs and incredible Amsterdam Flower Market. Dutch aquariums are very heavily planted, and the focus is mainly on the plants and not the fish. There may be few to no fish in a Dutch aquarium. The plants are commonly very lush, thus leaving little room for a high number of fishes. Dutch aquariums may not be as equipment intensive as some styles, but good lighting, filtration, and heating are usually required. Often substrate heating is used. Additional carbon dioxide is often used now, but is not an absolute requirement.

The design of a Dutch aquarium is based on a concept developed by the Greeks around 500 B.C. Pythagoras and Euclid knew of the golden rectangle, and this concept has been used extensively in art and architecture. Many great paintings of the renaissance used the concept to set up the elements depicted. The general idea is to create a layout that has elements that naturally draw the eye. The rest of the design functions to support one or two main focal elements.

If you want to get into it, research the way to make a proper golden triangle. Warning: You will need to crank out some math to get it exactly "right." This is not a math book, so let's cheat a little. To find the "focal points" for your tank, first find the diagonal across the tank. Find the diagonal that goes from the front left corner to the right back corner. Then divide the length of the tank into five equal sections. Focal points are located at the intersection of the middle two divisions and the diagonal (see fig. 2-1). The front to back/left to right diagonal is used to create a sense of movement; you view the tank from left to right.

The focal point is the place in your tank to place something that is different from the rest of the tank. Pieces of driftwood, rocks, or a special specimen plant

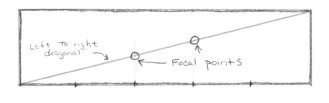

Fig. 2-1

are all items that work well as the focal point, though in a classic Dutch aquarium, usually a dramatic plant is used. Place plants that complement each other around the focal point(s). Use different colors by adding some red plants. Also use different plant textures to create interest. Place taller plants in the back of the tank and smaller plants in the front to create a tiered effect. Think of a Dutch tank as an impressionist painting where you use plants to create the scene.

The Nature Aquarium Style

Don't confuse this style with the natural aquarium that we talk about below. The natural aquarium style is credited to the world-renowned photographer Takashi Amano from Japan. This design was developed by Mr. Amano in the 1970s, and his style is best described as an underwater Japanese garden.

Some of the design elements found in this style and not found in others include the use of very small plants to create a carpet effect. The carpet may cover the substrate or objects within the tank. The use of aquatic mosses and liverworts like *Riccia* were introduced as carpeting plants in this style of tank. Many of the plants used require high light levels and the addition of CO_2 to thrive.

Often only a few plant species will commonly be used, as rocks and driftwood are often major focal points in the aquariums. They're used to create elements that mimic scenes found in nature. Rocks become mountains, while driftwood becomes a fallen tree in a moss garden. The animals are chosen to harmonize with the overall design.

The Nature Aquarium Style of Takashi Amano.

Similar to the Dutch aquariums, Amano uses classical art in his compositions, referring to the "golden section," a ratio of 1:1.618. Basically, this is the mathematical way to find the place where our eyes like to see things slightly off center to look correct. To make it easier, the ratio is about 3:5, as we discussed earlier when we were talking about Dutch aquariums.

The main difference between the two styles is in the materials they use around the point of interest. Where Dutch aquariums tend to fill in all the space with more plants, Amano's nature aquariums leave dramatic open spaces and use more elements of nature, such as rocks and branches.

The best way to become familiar with Amano's style is to purchase one of his books. The designs are fabulous, and the photography is outstanding. Many aquarists often emulate the Amano style.

Natural Aquariums

Though sometimes used to mean any planted aquarium, lately it is more often used to describe low-tech tanks. Generally these tanks use no or little filtration. To some, it may seem ironic to use such a great deal of technology to try to produce a little bit of nature. Loud aerators and filters are discarded. Often florescent lighting is used, but sometimes sunlight is the only source of light that is acceptable, as the idea is to use as many natural ingredients as possible.

These aquariums tend to be less formal in appearance than the higher-tech Dutch aquariums or Amano's nature aquariums. Natural aquariums have a more wild appearance, and often will house native fish, plants, and invertebrates. A natural aquarium strives to look like a more natural body of water in the wild. This is also a nice type of tank to have if you have a quite a few aquariums.

Biotope

The goal of a biotope aquarium is to re-create just a small piece of a natural body of water. Every attempt is made to select the correct water quality, gravel, plants or lack of plants, fish, and sometimes invertebrates that occupy a certain geographical area. Sometimes a biotope can re-create an algae-covered lake or even areas where there really is no true aquatic plant or plant-like life evident, so they don't even necessarily have to have plants in them. They can be a very interesting adventure and would certainly be fun to research.

The key to a good biotope tank is to be very consistent. Only use plants and animals that come from that exact environment. You should also strive to make the tank look like a window into that biotope. Popular biotopes include the Amazon River basin, mangrove swamps, African rift lakes, and North American cold-water lakes. Biotope displays are

Part 1

common in public aquariums. Use your imagination. That swampy little ditch on the side of the road is often a fascinating biotope that you could re-create in your aquarium.

Paludarium (Aquaterrarium)

The paludarium is a combination of a terrarium and aquarium. These setups can be truly awe inspiring. Since paludariums create a wet and humid environment, they are usually filled with beautiful water-loving plants that are difficult to grow otherwise. Ferns, mosses, and bromeliads are often the stars in paludariums. Pumps are often used to create waterfalls. A paludarium does require a lot of planning and initial construction, but it is certainly soothing and eye catching when done well.

When you design a paludarium, you can use elements of the Dutch, nature, or biotope styles. Use rocks, ledges, and wood to create natural-looking scenes. You could also choose a biotope to emulate–how about a Hawaiian waterfall?

Another Option

Paludariums (Aquaterrariums) are part terrarium and part aquarium. It's a fun style that can produce very dramatic results. And for more advanced fun, brackish and marine tanks can offer challenges for the planted aquarist, too.

Brackish

Brackish are probably the most difficult of the planted tanks. There are very few plants available that will tolerate the not totally fresh and not totally salt world of the brackish environment. Many plants can tolerate the small amount of salt that is sometimes recommended for fish, particularly in areas with soft water. The problem is that when you get up toward the half-and-half mark, there is not much in the way of freshwater plants or saltwater macroalgae that will survive. The best plant available to most hobbyists for such a setup is the *Cryptocoryne ciliata*. Brackish water fishes include mollies, some puffers, and archerfishes, just to name a few. Your local pet shop or fish dealer will be able to show you various species of other brackish-water fishes that may be desirable, too.

Marine

You can even take your planted aquarium hobby to the world of marine and reef aquariums. Many interesting macroalgae from the genus *Caulerpa* are relatively easy to grow, and there are quite a few species of the invertebrates that can be maintained in the reef tank as well. Some of these organisms require special lighting and strict maintenance

Part 1

Caulerpa can grow in marine aquariums.

standards, but *Caulerpa* can usually grow well with just standard florescent bulbs. In fact, these algae can grow to the point of being a nuisance and should be kept under control by pruning. Other species of macroalgae can also be grown, including some lovely dark-burgundy species.

Finding Your Supplies

It would really be nice if you could do one-stop shopping with this hobby, but it's more likely that you will need to shop around for just the right places to buy what you need. That's why it's important to distinguish the gems from the clinkers as you hop from store to store.

Some of you may live in more remote areas, like me. Take heart. You will soon discover the joys of catalog and Internet shopping. It is usually best, however, to go to your as-local-as-possible pet shop or aquarium dealer to pick your livestock out personally. You may need to take some road trips to various places around your county or state in order to find just the right addition for your

Finding a supplier for good livestock may require some traveling.

aquarium. Traveling has been one of the fun parts of the hobby for me. I (TAB) love going to aquarium stores, plumbing supply outlets, and garden shops to look for a new fish or plants.

The good news is that aquatic "gardening" is becoming more and more popular. As the demand grows, more retailers are carrying items for the aquatic plant hobby. You will find a good selection of chemicals, plants, and fish. Many items that could only be built from pieces from various sources are now available as ready-made units. There is also a variety of these items to choose from.

What to Avoid

First, you don't have to settle for limp plants, dead fish, and stinky water. If the plants are sickly, the water is smelly, and the fish look nasty, take your hard-earned dollars somewhere else. Of course it is a matter of degrees, but if a place looks shabby, it probably does not take good care of its stock. Imagine buying a plant that just continues to wither despite your best efforts, or worse, bringing home a diseased fish to infect your whole aquarium. Disaster!

However, a new aquarium keeper may see some situations that look bad but really aren't. For example, a water plant display at a dealer that has water like pea soup is not necessarily bad. The grower has probably recently fertilized the water plants, and the algae is having a field day. Are the plants nice and green, with new growth evident? If yes, you are probably looking at some good stuff.

Avoid the cheap stuff as well. Buy the best quality items that your budget will allow. This applies not only to fish and plants, but to aquarium hardware too. Some items may be inexpensive to purchase but will wear out quickly and cost you more in the long run. We will point out these potential problems when we discuss each hardware item. Since you are new to this, however, it will be more difficult at first to determine the best names in hardware. Shop around and ask like-minded people for ideas and advice.

Water Plants

Many aquarium stores now carry a large selection of aquatic plants. First look at the overall appearance of the plant. Does it have many dead and dying leaves? A few dead or dying leaves may be normal for many water plants, because they shed the old leaves and grow new ones. But any dealer worth his salt will take the time to properly prune the plants and remove dying leaves. If the plant has a few not-so-good leaves and lots of new growth, it's probably in good shape.

Next, lift the plant out of the water. Bare root plants should have healthy roots and new roots starting from the base of the plant. For potted plants, inspect the container or pot it is in. Does it look overcrowded like it's exploding from the pot? Are there any signs that the roots are rotting? Don't bother buying plants that aren't in good shape; even the best green thumb may not be able to save something that is going downhill.

Fake Aquatic Plants

You do need to know a little about plants before you go shopping for them. Take a look at the plant section of this book before you start shopping. Many retailers will have "fake" plants for sale. Actually, they are real plants, but they were never meant to be underwater. There are a few terrestrial plants that will be all right underwater for a little while, but they never grow and eventually die when submerged. My advice is to not even bother with them.

Common Imposters

Here is a list of plants that you may find for sale as aquatic plants. They are not true aquatic plants, however, and are not able to be submerged for long periods of time, so please don't buy them for your aquarium.

Umbrella Pine	Peace Lily
Mondo Grass, Fountain Plant	Underwater Palm
Spider Plant	Chinese Evergreen
Club Mosses	Sandriana, Green Dragon Plant
Aluminum Plant	Arrowhead

Emerged Growth

Some aquarium plants may have been grown emerged, with their leaves out of the water. The plant will be strong and healthy but may need time to adjust to life as a submerged plant. The plant may even need to grow new leaves that are better adapted to the lower light and CO_2 levels found in water. There is nothing wrong with growing many aquatic plants this way. Many species are normally found in areas that flood–time out of the water may be normal.

Gone Fishing

Finding good-quality aquarium fish has become harder. Your success will largely depend on the popularity of the hobby in your area. We have had the hardest time finding anything but the most common aquarium fish in local stores. When I have my heart set on something different, then the shopping begins.

Only buy fish that look healthy, happy, and bright. How do you tell? The fish should not be hanging around on the sides or bottom of its tank. It should have no damage to its fins or scales. If there is a dead fish in the tank, pass on all of them.

Hardware

In most cases, buying tanks somewhere local will be the least expensive for you. You will avoid shipping costs this way. Let the retailer handle the shipping to your local area; this is especially true with glass tanks. You may also want to consider buying used tanks. Many people enter the hobby halfheartedly or don't stick with it and will give you a good price on used items.

Add-on items like filters, lights, CO_2 systems, and other small items can be purchased through mail-order sources quite easily should your local pet shop not have it for you. You may even save some money. Just make sure that you plan out your aquarium so that you will have all the items that you want before you set up your tank.

Where to Find Your Stuff

Finding your aquarium supplies can make you into a treasure seeker. Let's discuss the pros and cons of each place to buy your supplies. I'm going to give you my general opinion of each outlet, but remember that there will be good ones and bad ones in each category. Use your best shopping skills to find the best quality for the money.

Pet Stores

Pet stores are the best place to look for fish and some plants. Even in a pet store that sells all kinds of things (full line), the fish department often makes up a large percentage of sales. You may get lucky and find members of the staff that know fish. There are different types of pet stores to consider.

Hometown Pet Shops

Hometown shops are the small neighborhood pet stores. They will usually carry supplies that appeal to the interests of the owner. You are in luck, though. The aquarium hobby is widespread, and you are bound to find a hometown shop that caters to the fish crowd.

For plants, hometown shops will likely carry some plants for tropical aquariums. The hobby is growing, so you may even find a small retailer who carries a great selection. You may even end up bringing some back to your retailer for trade.

Another point about hometown shops: They will probably be willing to special-order items for you. These will be the most flexible dealers you will find. If you find a good local small retailer, you have found gold.

Pet Superstores

Pet superstores carry many common tropical fish. The fish are typically kept in large central systems. If one tank has problems with disease, they all will, because all of the tanks are connected. Some do a great job with the fish, and some do not. Be choosy, and remember to quarantine fish before putting them in your tank. Most will also have a fairly generous return policy—just keep the dead bodies. I have purchased fish from these outlets with mostly favorable results. It probably depends on the expertise of the store's staff.

You may be able to collect your own plants in some areas.

Collecting Your Own Specimens

I have collected a few water lilies and oxygenating plants this way. I want to caution you that collecting wild specimens may be illegal in some areas. There are also plants that cannot be transported across state lines. That's because some water plants can become so noxious that they clog waterways and ponds. Others may be rare and protected. Be sure to check with your state and federal wildlife officials for a complete list of legal and illegal plant and animal species in your area.

The plants you collect may also be unable to tolerate the much warmer water they will often find in your aquarium. This will be especially true of any plant removed from a stream. If you collect wild specimens, make sure that they can survive the conditions of your tank.

Make a rule to disturb the habitat as little as possible. Root around as little as you can get away with to remove the plant. You will also have to muck about in some really gooey mud beds. Most likely, you can bypass the leeches and get a better specimen at your favorite retailer.

Part Two

Aquarium Science

Fish Anthropologists

All About Water

Water is amazing stuff! From a chemist's point of view, it is a very unique substance. Did you know that it is nearly impossible to make absolutely pure water? It is a great solvent, and there are all sorts of things dissolved in most water. Water is polar–that means that it has an electrical charge that helps it attract other molecules (which is what happens when things dissolve). The electrical charge also creates water's physical properties, such as surface tension.

You probably feel like you're back in science class at this point. All you wanted was to grow nice plants and keep a few fish, and now we are getting very technical. However, a basic understanding of the science behind your hobby will help you in

A quality planted tank begins with quality water.

The ideas in this chapter will be expanded later in the book. Be sure to read all the sections to get the most benefit from this chapter.

the long run. You will be able to understand the cause of the problems you may have in your tank and then be able to make a plan for improvement. Planted-aquarium enthusiasts need to understand these concepts just a little better. For high-tech tanks, you will need to control these water conditions much more than the average aquarist. We will go into how all of this affects your planted tank in Chapter 6. First, let's get grounded in the basics.

Let's Start with pH

The scale that is used to measure whether water is acidic or basic is referred to as pH, and it is read as a number on a scale from 1 to 14. The low numbers are acid and the high numbers are base. Seven is neutral. What exactly does that mean?

Well pH is best described as a measurement of the hydrogen ions that are floating around in water. An ion is a charged molecule or atom. In the case of hydrogen (H+), it has a positive charge. That means it would love to snap up an electron (which has a negative charge) from some other chemical. That's a chemical reaction. That is why acids burn your skin. They snatch away all the electrons from your skin and break it down.

The term "pH" is always spelled with a lowercase p and a capital H. It comes from the German "potenz power + H (symbol for hydrogen)"

Similarly, a basic solution (that's "basic," as in "the opposite of acidic") does not have many hydrogen ions but has plenty of hydroxyl ions (OH^-). Hydroxyl ions like to react too. They are looking for positive ions to combine with. Drain-cleaning chemicals are usually made of lye, or sodium hydroxide (NaOH), which is as basic as you can get. Strong bases like lye react with just about everything.

The pH scale is logarithmic. That means that if you go from a pH of 7 to 8, you have actually increased alkalinity tenfold. The main reason you need to know this is because a one-point change in pH can be much more drastic than you think. A single increase in pH from 7 to 8, for example, means that your water is now 10 times more basic than before.

pH for Planted Tanks

You can easily test the pH of your water by buying a test kit, which you can find at any pet supply store. Most of them have a vial that you fill with water from your aquarium.

You then add a pill or a few drops of liquid. Wait a little while for a chemical reaction to take place. Your water will turn a color, just like magic. All that is left to do is compare your color with the color chart that came in the kit. You can also find tests that use little strips that you dip in the water. They are okay, but the ones with the vials are more accurate. You can also buy pH test kits that zero in on a certain pH range.

A variety of test kits are available to measure the important chemical properties of your tank.

Neutral pH is usually best for aquarium fishes and plants. Remember, that is a pH of around 7, but this also depends on some other chemical properties of your tank. We will put this all together later on in this chapter.

Changing Your pH

Before you ever fill your aquarium, you should first check the pH of the water that comes out of your tap. This way, you'll know if the water is safe to use straight out of the tap. The majority of the time, the normal pH of your house water is fine for your aquarium. You can usually just use your water at the pH of your tap water when you fill your new aquarium and for any water changes, unless your tap water is extremely acidic or basic.

I think it is better to fool around with the water only if it is really needed. In the case of water that has very high pH (over 8) or low pH (below 6.5), you may need to make some adjustments. Later we will discuss changes in pH of your tank, why they occur, and what (if anything) you should do about it.

Down You Go

Lowering the pH in your aquarium can be a difficult task. It is much easier to raise the pH. I tend to be a conservative aquarium keeper and try to deal with the natural situation. If the pH is not over 7.5, I recommend just watching it. If it climbs higher, start looking at your rocks. You may have rocks in your aquarium that drive the pH up naturally.

You can test your rocks by placing them in a bucket of the water that you use for the aquarium and letting it soak. Test the pH before you add the rock and then again a week or two later. Did the pH go up? Your rock is the culprit.

Part 2

At a high pH (over 8), ammonia becomes more toxic to your fish. When you test for ammonia, test for pH too!

Your fish will adapt to your water and will usually have no problems if the pH is somewhere in the range of 6.5 to 8, as constant fiddling with the pH is more stressful to fish in the long run.

At high pH values, the ammonia is much more toxic. The only time I would worry about the pH that is a little high is when cycling your aquarium. You may need to do extra water changes and be vigilant with your test kit while you cycle a high pH tank.

To lower your pH, make very small adjustments each day, and test the water before and after you add chemicals to the aquarium. Here are some suggestions for lowering pH:

• Use commercially available pH adjustment chemicals. It is very important to buy products that *do not* add phosphates to the water. Excess phosphates will aggravate an algae bloom. You should note, though, that using chemicals may not give the best results.

• Use a reverse osmosis unit to remove the minerals from your water that contribute to the high pH. However, you will want to add back a portion of tap water or add buffering chemicals to optimize the water.

• Use peat to create acidic "black water." Most of you will probably not want to go this route. "Black water" is more often used for breeding certain species of fish or for creating a more authentic Amazon-basin biotope aquarium.

• Collect rain water for your tanks. Many aquarists who desire lower pH water have very good results with rain water. However, there can be some problems with collecting rain water, too. Rain water can contain pollutants that were in the air when the rain was falling, the kind of situation that leads to acid rain. Be sure to let the first rain fall to the ground and don't start collecting until the rain has a chance to clean the air a bit. Also be careful about collecting water that runs off your roof, as it may have dirt or pollutants in it too, wait until the roof has a chance to get clean before you start collecting.

Raising the pH
Many plants do well in, and may actually prefer somewhat acidic water but you may have

water with too low of a pH. This is more common when you get your water from a well. Acidic water is also usually soft, meaning it lacks minerals and carbonates. You may also find that the pH of the water in your aquarium may become more acidic over time. This is caused by the natural breakdown of leaves and other organic materials in the water. I think it is a good idea to increase the pH of acidic water to neutral, as needed. It is very easy to increase the pH:

• If the acidity has developed over time, change your water more often. A 10 percent water change twice a week should help quickly. This is the easiest thing in the world to do.

• Add a little baking soda to your water. Only add 1 teaspoon for every 10 gallons. Make all pH changes slowly.

• Use a commercial pH adjustment buffer to raise the pH of your water. Follow the directions included with the product and look for phosphate-free buffers.

Liquid Rocks—Water Hardness

You may be familiar with the idea of hard water because of the deposits you see in your bathtub. Water is an excellent solvent, and your water will have more or less minerals dissolved in it, depending on where you live.

You can measure the hardness of your water. General hardness is a measure of calcium and magnesium ions in the water. You will commonly see the units of measurement for general hardness as degrees of general hardness (dGH or DH). Hardness can also be measured in ppm–parts per million (ppm). You can easily convert from one to the other by multiplying dGH by 17.9 to get ppm (or dividing ppm by 17.9 to get dGH).

If you have a water-softener unit, the best thing to do is bypass the softener for water used in your aquarium. Whole-house water softeners remove the calcium and magnesium ions, replacing them with sodium. Excess sodium is harmful to your plants.

Alkalinity and Carbonate Hardness

There are two basic types of water hardness. I've already talked about general hardness. The second type is carbonate hardness, which is most often very nearly equal to the alkalinity of the water.

Carbonate Hardness

This refers to the amount of carbonate $(CO_3)^{2-}$ and bicarbonate $(HCO_3)^-$ ions in the water. You are probably familiar with the acid-neutralizing properties of bicarbonates such as baking soda. There is the old remedy for an acidic stomach of a glass of water with a little baking soda (sodium bicarbonate) in it. Nasty but effective.

Alkalinity is a measure of the ability of your water to buffer or stabilize itself when there are acids that can change the pH of the water. The acids react with the carbonates to keep the pH from going down. The carbonate and bicarbonate ions make up a large part of the molecules that contribute to alkalinity. (The acids react with the carbonates to keep the pH from going down to the extent that carbonate hardness and alkalinity are used as interchangeable terms). I think this is especially confusing for new aquarists. It is possible to have other components, like sulfates, that contribute to alkalinity. In most cases, the alkalinity will be nearly equal to the carbonate hardness. This is a very important point for the beginning aquarist. Your alkalinity test kit will measure the *total* alkalinity, carbonates, etc. You will see later on why you are more interested in the carbonates, so my advice is to take the small margin of error by considering your measured KH (alkalinity) equal to carbonate hardness.

Your test kit will probably express the results as degrees KH (dKH or KH), but you may also see references in metric units of milliequivalents per liter (abbreviated meq/L), or the English scale of parts per million (expressed as ppm $CaCO_3$–$CaCO_3$ is the carbonate). To convert from dKH to ppm, just multiply by 17.9.

General Hardness

This refers to the minerals calcium and magnesium in your water. This type of hardness is important to the fish. Some fish do best in water with more or less of these minerals present. Most aquarists will be fine with water that comes from the tap. Some fish will not breed well unless the water is very soft or hard, but unless you are especially interested in breeding certain fish, don't worry.

Alkalinity

This refers to the ability of your water to handle pH swings. In a planted tank, the gas carbon dioxide will be the main component of these pH swings. We will talk about that next. One topic builds on the next. Our goal is to put everything together so that you can optimize your aquarium water for your plants and fish.

If your water has naturally low carbonate hardness, your aquarium may have trouble staying at a stable pH. You will probably also notice that the pH is also a little low. The remedy is the same for raising the pH. Your best bet is to add a little baking soda.

Gasses in your Aquarium

There will also be dissolved gasses in your aquarium that are the byproducts of the respiration of both the plants and the fish. Oxygen and CO_2 are the two gasses present that you need to know about.

Carbon Dioxide

CO_2 is one of the dissolved gases that will end up in your water. But I want to talk about CO_2 as a special case. CO_2 is given off by your fish and by your plants at night. In an aquarium, this fact can lead to some unexpected problems. The interactions of CO_2 and water are fairly complicated. Did you notice how close carbonate (CO_3) and carbon dioxide (CO_2) are chemically? Carbon dioxide interacts with the carbonate system of your water (the alkalinity).

The carbonate system is the most complicated in your aquarium, so let's just hit some of the highlights:

• When the water is acidic (pH below 6), dissolved CO_2 is most prevalent.

• When the water is neutral (pH 7 to 8), dissolved CO_2 is mainly converted to bicarbonates.

• When the water is very alkaline (pH 10), dissolved CO_2 is mostly in the form of carbonates.

• The carbonates can react with calcium and precipitate out of solution in the case of high pH, which will lower the carbonate hardness of the water. If you see white particles in your tank, this is what happened. Calcium carbonate is not very soluble in water–it can be formed as a white solid in your tank.

Here is the most important point for you: CO_2 can lower the pH. If there is calcium carbonate present, it is dissolved by the more acidic water, and the pH can go back up. It may take a little time, though.

The dissolved CO_2 affects the entire chemical system of the aquarium water. What does that mean to you, the average aquarium keeper? Let's talk about one more topic, then I'll put it all together.

Plant Respiration

Do you remember that huge word "photosynthesis"? Photosynthesis is the process by which plants use light and CO_2 to make sugar. They give off oxygen when they are using the carbon dioxide. But the sun only shines for part of the day! If light is the key ingredient of photosynthesis, what do plants do when it is dark?

Answer: They use up oxygen. Whoa! Who knew?

Stirring the Pot

Let's put it all together now. Plants use CO_2 in the day and give off oxygen. At night the process is reversed: they use oxygen and give off CO_2. You have a situation now where both the plants and animals are giving off CO_2.

Life in the Big City

What this all means is that the pH in your aquarium can and probably will vary throughout the day. If you measure your pH at several different times during the day and didn't know about this, wouldn't you start to worry? The pH of your aquarium will be lower in the early morning. If you measure pH at this time, you will probably be tempted to make unnecessary adjustments.

Instead, wait until afternoon to measure the pH, and make changes slowly and cautiously. If your water has adequate alkalinity, the natural pH swing will be mild and will have no effect on your animals and plants.

The Nitrogen Cycle

We have already discussed the basic chemistry of your planted aquarium. In this chapter, we will talk about a very important biological process that deals with the wastes created by fishes and other living things in aquariums. Mother Nature, you see, is really wonderful. This natural system works to keep the water in your aquarium clean and safe for your fish— it is called the nitrogen cycle.

Have you ever thought about what it's like to be a fish? You swim, you eat, and you poop. And you do it all in the same water. *Gross*! How is it possible to keep fish in a closed environment like an aquarium, then? You would think that eventually they would be poisoned in their own

The nitrogen cycle plays an important role in your success as an aquarist.

waste. Well, this could happen, if you were a careless fish keeper. But I know you aren't. And now you'll find out how you can use the nitrogen cycle to your advantage and create a nice home for your fish.

Ammonia

Fish produce nitrogen waste in the form of ammonia. Nitrogen waste is a by-product of protein digestion. We all need protein to live, and we need a way to be rid of the excess nitrogen that results from its digestion. Our bodies convert the ammonia to urea, but fish excrete most of their ammonia directly from their gills into the water. They also excrete urine, which contains small amounts of urea as well.

All the advice in this chapter applies to an aquarium, a bucket, and even the plastic bag that you use to bring your new fish home in.

You have probably encountered ammonia as a household cleaner. Ever take a whiff from that bottle? It's horrible and poisonous. It wouldn't take long for an aquarium full of fish to excrete so much ammonia that they are poisoned in their own waste. If you had too many fish and not enough water, this could get out of hand fast.

Bacteria to the Rescue

By now you may be wondering how fish survive at all in an aquarium. The answer is bacteria. A healthy aquarium will establish a large population of bacteria that love to eat ammonia. There is also another type of bacteria that takes the waste from the ammonia lovers and converts it again into a nontoxic form of nitrogen. Both of these types of bacteria live on surfaces inside the aquarium. They live on the rocks, the sides of the tank, and on the sparkly cave you bought for your new fishes. Most good aquarium filters provide a lot of surface area for these bacteria to colonize.

The problem is that when you set up a new aquarium, the good bacteria have not had time to establish colonies in the tank. In other words, a sterile aquarium can be deadly to your fish. I know this might seem counterintuitive, but there are good bacteria and bad bacteria—and the good bacteria are absolutely essential for the survival of your fish. If you add too many fish too fast to a new aquarium, you are asking for disaster. You need to give the good bacteria time to colonize your system. They are all over everything anyway (isn't nature grand?) and will grow in response to the ammonia produced by your fish. The only thing you need to do now is wait.

Egad, More Chemistry!

Isn't this the best science project you ever worked on? There is a whole lot of science behind the aquarium hobby. Let's get more specific about the nitrogen cycle now.

If you use a water test kit to measure the progress of the nitrogen cycle (which I definitely recommend), you will first see the ammonia level in your aquarium go up. You may actually see your fish become distressed as the level of ammonia increases. If you have added many fish or very large fish to a brand new aquarium, the ammonia level can get too high in just one day. This is why you are not going to add too many fish or very large fish to a new aquarium, right?

What about all that ammonia? The first step in the nitrogen cycle is accomplished by bacteria called nitrosomonas and nitrobacter. These bacteria convert ammonia (NH_3) to nitrite (NO_2). It will take about a week for them to multiply and start eating up the ammonia. The ammonia level starts to drop as the bacteria kick into high gear. Whew! Just in time.

We're not done yet. The problem is that nitrite is still toxic to fish, although it's not as bad as ammonia. Mother Nature to the rescue again! The nitrospira bacteria will convert that nitrite (NO_2) to nitrate (NO_3). The good news is that nitrate is not harmful to your fish. You will take care of some of that with partial water changes.

Nitrosomas and nitrobacter are called aerobic bacteria. That means they need oxygen to do their job. It is easy to see from the chemical formula that they add oxygen to the nitrogen. When the nitrosomas converts ammonia (NH_3) to nitrite (NO_2), you can see that oxygen has to be added. And converting nitrite (NO_2) to nitrate (NO_3) requires yet more oxygen.

> ### Testing, testing...
> A good investment for your aquarium is a test kit that you can use to measure the ammonia, nitrite, and nitrate levels in the water. The nitrate level is not critical to monitor because it is not toxic to your fish, but monitoring the ammonia and nitrite is very important.

Part 2

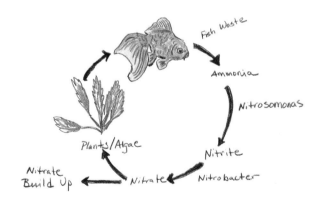

Nitrogen Cycle

Fig. 5.1

How to Cycle Your New Aquarium

You will be rewarded by being patient with the way you add fish and other animals to your aquarium. Let's assume that your substrate is in the tank. You should also have your filter and lights running.

For a new tank, I recommend that you just recirculate water through your filter system for at least a week before you begin to add any fish. You can use this time to make sure everything is working perfectly. You can also add more plants or move them around during this time. Certain materials that can be used in the substrate may need some time to settle out. Testing the water for baseline levels of pH, ammonia, and nitrite is also a good idea.

Discus are good candidates for the cycled aquatic garden.

You can begin to add your plants to your aquarium when you are confident that there are no mechanical problems (filters and lights) or water-quality surprises. The more plants that you add before fish, the better. Plants will mitigate some of the effects of the nitrogen cycle when you add fish. They will also be covered in good bacteria that will help seed your aquarium. It is best to add a full complement of plants to your aquarium at the start. This will reduce algae problems later.

If you absolutely can't wait and have been admiring a special fish, go ahead and buy one. Just one. If you're looking at small fish and you have a larger aquarium, you can get away with three or four at the most. I recommend that you buy some small tetras to start cycling your aquarium. Neon tetras are very common in pet stores and look great in most planted aquariums. They are usually not too expensive, either.

After you add the first few fish, measure the ammonia and nitrite levels of the aquarium every day. You will first see ammonia and no nitrite. As the ammonia level gets higher, the nitrite levels will begin to register. The ammonia levels will start to drop off as the nitrite levels increase. If you decide to measure nitrate, you will see the nitrate levels slowly begin to rise as the nitrite levels fall. You do not need to monitor the nitrate levels, but do keep monitoring until you see both ammonia and nitrite levels fall to zero.

In a very large aquarium with only one or two small fish, you may not be able to measure the ammonia or nitrite levels at all. However, your aquarium still needs time to grow beneficial bacteria, so you still need to be patient. As you add more fish, or if you add a large fish, the ammonia levels may rise again as more bacteria grow to deal with the additional ammonia, but the spike should not last very long. It is best to add additional fish only a few at a time.

Cycling Problems

There can be problems as you cycle your aquarium. Maybe you weren't patient enough. Maybe you overestimated how many fish you could add at one time. You can also see problems if you have moved fish to a temporary tank where there is no filter or you have a new filter. (Remember, a new filter does not yet have a thriving colony of good bacteria to deal with ammonia and nitrite.)

How do you know there is a problem? Two simple ways. The first and most accurate way is to test for ammonia and nitrite. Measure them frequently! This is the best way to get a feeling for the condition of your water.

You may also have a problem if your fish begin to behave strangely or look sickly. Ammonia toxicity can make the fish lethargic. Finally, the fish might start to flash repeatedly. Flashing is a common fish behavior. Flashing occurs when a fish flips on its side to scratch against something. They may do it because they are itchy. They may also do it because their skin is very irritated by bad water quality or parasites. If you see many fish flashing, or one that flashes repeatedly, investigate the cause of the behavior.

Ammonia Fixes

There are several things you can do to help your fish if you are experiencing high ammonia levels. When you have confirmed with your handy test kit that there is a problem, your immediate attention is needed. If the ammonia level is creeping up a little, don't panic. You need some ammonia in the water for the good bacteria to start

> **...and more testing**
>
> Test your test kits. Use your tap water to become familiar with how your test kit works. You get to practice, and you can also measure the different water-quality parameters of your water. You may find that your tap water is not great and is the source of unsatisfactory readings from your aquarium.

Part 2

> *The unit measurement "ppm" stands for parts per million.*

multiplying. Confirm that the level is too high before you take steps. Your test kit will indicate what level of ammonia is too high.

The most immediate and simple thing you can do is change the water. You may even see your fish get right into the stream of the hose for relief. Make sure you are adding good water to the aquarium, though, so you don't make your problem worse. If you have already determined that your local water needs to be treated before it goes into the aquarium, then do so. For high ammonia, a 50 percent water change is a good idea.

Another option is to add a liquid ammonia remover. These products react with the ammonia to make the water, and the ammonia in it, less toxic to your aquarium inhabitants. You definitely do not want to rely on a product like this to solve a chronic ammonia problem, but it is an excellent first-aid measure. Also consider putting these products in the bag or container that you use to bring your fish home in, because some act as stress relievers as well.

A second option is to use zeolite chips in your chemical filter chamber. Zeolite is a mineral that absorbs ammonia from the water. It looks like white gravel but is porous and soaks up the ammonia molecules. It takes about 1 gram of zeolite to remove 1.5 milligrams of ammonia. Let me translate that for you. You will need 25 grams (0.13 lb) of zeolite to remove 1 ppm of ammonia from 10 gallons of water. Use this ratio to determine the amount of zeolite that you will need for your particular situation.

Don't Fall In

Zeolite cannot bind ammonia very well in the presence of salt. If you have added salt to your aquarium and have an ammonia problem, zeolite will not work well for you. Use a liquid ammonia remover instead.

Zeolite will stop working when it has absorbed as much ammonia as it can hold. You can recharge the spent zeolite by soaking it in a solution of salt and water, then rinsing it and drying it. You can probably get three or four uses. Do not recharge it by adding salt to your aquarium, because it will let go of all that ammonia it was holding. Disaster!

Mesh laundry bags are excellent containers for zeolite. You can move the bags into your filter box as needed. When you go to a koi show, you will probably see a little bag of white gravel in each tank. Now you know what it is and what it is used for.

The Basics

- Naturally occurring bacteria break down ammonia and nitrite.
- Don't put too many fish in your aquarium too soon.
- You can add plants at any time.
- Test to be sure that everything is okay before you start adding more fish.
- The nitrogen cycle will take two to three weeks. Be patient!
- Resist the urge to mess too much with your aquarium's chemistry. Let nature take its course.

Finally, to fix an ammonia problem, you can lower the pH of the water to around 6.8. Ammonia is much more toxic at a high pH. If your aquarium pH has gone up past 8, ammonia can be especially toxic.

Nitrite Knock-Outs

The *Nitrosomonas* bacteria have kicked in and are changing the ammonia to nitrite. Nitrite is still toxic to your fish, and the nitrobacter is now ready to do its job. But it is going to take time for the second-shift bacteria to colonize the filter and get busy with the nitrite. What can you do if the nitrite levels get too high in the meantime?

You are testing your water, right? If the nitrite is too high, the best thing to do is change about 20 percent of the aquarium water. Resist the urge to toss in a lot of chemicals; changing water should be your first choice. You need some of the offending ammonia or nitrite present in the water for the good bacteria to live on as they multiply and colonize your aquarium. If you completely remove the bad stuff, you will just postpone the inevitable–a healthy, well-cycled aquarium.

Keep checking your nitrate levels daily and change another 20 percent of the water as needed. Soon you should see the nitrate levels drop to nothing.

Bacteria Buddies

A quick look in an aquarium magazine and you will see products advertised that are solutions or powders of the good-guy bacteria. The worst thing that could happen by adding one of these products to your aquarium is that you waste some money. The potential benefit is that you will populate your filter with good bacteria faster.

You could also try adding one of these products if you are having a cycling problem. The bacteria may not start to work fast enough to help your fish, so don't forget to use other methods as well–especially partial water changes. Just remember that you can get these bacteria for free if you are patient and cycle your aquarium slowly.

The Tortoise and the Hare

The nitrogen cycle will take some time to start working in your aquarium, and the temperature needs to be at least 60°F in order for the process to be initialized in most planted aquariums. Since most planted tanks are kept in the low to mid 70s, temperature issues should be rare. Some ammonia and some nitrite must be present to feed the growing bacteria. There is really nothing you can do to make it happen any faster. Just keep testing the water every few days and let nature take its course.

The best approach is to just go through the cycle with a small fish load, and you should have no problems at all. I have told you how to solve problems should they arise, but don't think you have to do anything just because you measure some ammonia and nitrite. Be sure that you have a problem before you act. You and your fish should cycle along just fine if you watch carefully and choose the simplest actions first.

6

Advanced Planted Tank Chemistry

The previous two chapters gave you the basics for a good aquarist. Let's take things a little further. You may ask, "Why?" What is the point of delving deeper into these chemistry topics? Hey, I can tell you! Even if it takes a while to understand, knowing these things can help you to solve problems you may encounter with confidence and the ability to analyze and then solve the problem. That is science in action–observe, test, understand, and solve.

In this chapter, we will talk more about the chemistry of carbon dioxide (CO_2) in the planted aquarium, specifically the addition of additional CO_2 to your planted tank. First, know that you can grow beautiful water plants without adding

Taking time to learn some water chemistry will improve your chances of having a tank like this.

Carbon dioxide is important for flourishing planted aquariums.

CO_2. To get truly show-quality results, however, you will need to go with CO_2. There is also a way to ease into using CO_2 that I will also tell you about. I want you to understand what will happen to your water chemistry when you add CO_2.

Second, we will talk about the use of fertilizers and the nutrients beyond the CO_2 and light that plants need. Once again, you don't need to be picky about these things to get some nice results, but dosing specific nutrients can improve your results.

Why Add CO$_2$ Anyway?

Animal and plant metabolism is interestingly complementary. We breathe in oxygen (O_2) and CO_2. Plants "breathe" in CO_2 and give off O_2 in the presence of light (energy). Plants make it possible for animals to exist on this basic level–they make good food, too.

The building block of life is carbon. Our tissues, bones, and bodies are made up of all sorts of carbon-based chemicals that do a million different tasks in the body. Plants are no different. We get our carbon from the food we take in. Plants can't eat, so they need to "breathe" in their carbon in the form of CO_2.

In the case of aquatic plants, they have the added burden of respiring CO_2 from water. The amount of CO_2 in air averages about 340 ppm. In water, CO_2 levels are low, 0 to 4 ppm. Aquatic plants are well adapted to absorbing CO_2–they have to be!

Here is another subtlety to your new hobby. The plants that you choose to grow have tens of thousands of years of evolution behind them and are well adapted to their environments. By moving them into an aquarium, you are often putting them in an "unnatural" condition.

Some plants are truly aquatic–all phases of their life are spent underwater. The rest have evolved with varying degrees of "wetness." Some grow on the margin of bodies of water–half in, half out. Some may only be submerged for part of a season, like the seasonal flooding of the Amazon Basin. Some may be adapted to clinging to a rock on the edge of a fast-moving stream. Water lilies send all of their leaves up to the surface! Your aquatic plants will naturally have differing abilities for getting CO_2 from your aquarium water.

Another important fact is that many aquarium plants are actually not raised underwater! They are grown with their leaves immersed to get them to market faster and healthier. These plants will need time to adapt to life underwater in your tank. So the fact is that some of your plants will simply do better if they have more CO_2 around.

How about figuring out a way to get more CO_2 to your water plants? Great idea! Adding CO_2 helps plants grow faster simply because they have much more of their basic nutrient.

Big CO_2 Water Chemistry

Okay, here we go. The three things that are most important here are the ideas of pH, KH, and CO_2 interaction. Let's review what we already know.

• pH measures the amount of hydrogen ions in the tank–this tells you if the water is acidic or basic. Low pH is acidic. A high pH is considered basic, and adding CO_2 will only make your water more acidic and thus lower the pH value.

• KH measures the amount of alkalinity in the tank–this is the power the water has to balance itself when acids are formed in the tank. The KH determines how fast and how much the pH in your tank can change–this is important. KH is the only one of these properties that will not change! For this discussion, let's assume that KH is close enough to carbonate hardness. If you buffer with any phosphates, this all goes out the window!

Carbon dioxide is just one factor in solid water chemistry.

• CO_2 will dissolve in water that is more basic and has higher KH. You will need a moderate amount of carbonate hardness in your water to get good performance with injected CO_2.

The pH/KH/CO$_2$ Table

This chart shows you the relationship between pH, KH, and CO$_2$. It can give you a good scientific understanding of the chemistry going on in your tank. Don't become intimidated; just look over the chart and try to get a feel for the numbers.

CO$_2$ Concentration (ppm)

pH / KH	6.0	6.2	6.4	6.6	6.8	7.0	7.2	7.4	7.6	7.8	8.0
0.5	15	9.3	5.9	3.7	2.4	1.5	0.93	0.59	0.37	0.24	0.15
1.0	30	18.6	11.8	7.4	4.7	3.0	1.7	1.2	0.74	0.47	0.30
1.5	44	28	17.6	11.1	7.0	4.4	2.8	1.8	1.11	0.70	0.44
2.0	59	37	24	14.8	9.4	5.9	3.7	2.4	1.48	0.94	0.59
2.5	73	46	30	18.5	11.8	7.3	4.6	3.0	1.85	1.18	0.73
3.0	87	56	35	22	14.0	8.7	5.6	3.5	2.2	1.40	0.87
3.5	103	65	41	26	16.4	10.3	6.5	4.1	2.6	1.64	1.03
4.0	118	75	47	30	18.7	11.8	7.5	4.7	3.0	1.87	1.18
5.0	147	93	59	37	23	14.7	9.3	5.9	3.7	2.3	1.47
6.0	177	112	71	45	28	17.7	11.2	7.1	4.5	2.8	1.77
8.0	240	149	94	59	37	24	14.9	9.4	5.9	3.7	2.4
10.0	300	186	118	74	47	30	18.6	11.8	7.4	4.7	3.0
15.0	440	280	176	111	70	44	28	17.6	11.1	7.0	4.4
20.0	590	370	240	148	94	59	37	24	14.8	9.4	5.9

How to Use This Table

To find the amount of CO$_2$ dissolved in your water, measure the pH and the KH. Find your pH and KH on the chart. The number in the table where they intersect will be very close to the CO$_2$ level in your tank.

Another way to use the chart is to decide which water parameters you want to use in your tank.

1. Pick Your pH–Let the type of fish and plants be your guide. Most fish will do fine at a neutral pH of 7.0.

2. Pick Your Desired CO_2 Level–10 to 20 ppm is a good range for plant growth. Excess CO_2 will kill your fish! I have read any number of upper limits to CO_2 to prevent poisoning your fish. To be safe, use 20 ppm as a good high number, but don't go over 25ppm.

3. Adjust the KH of the Tank Water–One really easy way to do this is plan on adjusting the KH of all water used to change water. Make initial adjustments to your tank, then to any water you add later.

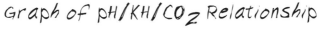

Graph of pH/KH/CO₂ Relationship

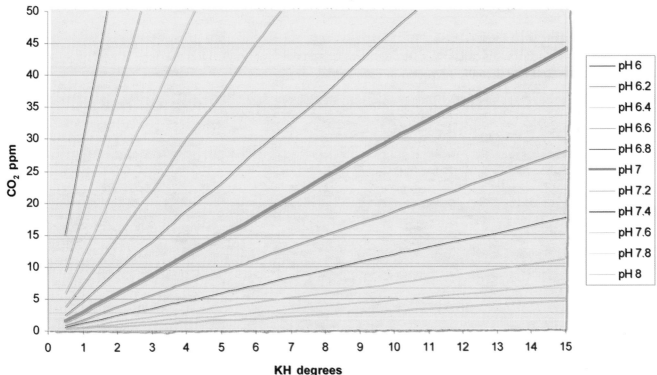

Example: Let's say that you want to run at pH 7.0 and about 20 ppm of CO_2 (that's a little high but I am going to grow some really CO_2-hungry plants). I go to the pH 7.0 line, then travel down until I see a number close to 20. At a KH of 6.0, I see that the CO_2 ppm is around 17.7. That is close enough for me, so I will adjust the KH of my water to 6.0 degrees.

How to Use the Graph

There are two ways that you can use this graph. Both are easy and will help you understand what may happen in your new planted aquarium.

First, you can use the graph just like the chart. Use it to help you decide a KH and pH to get your desired CO_2 range. Second, you can use it to predict what will happen to the pH in your tank if you turn off the CO_2. On the graph, find your KH and your pH (with CO_2 on). Just follow the line at the KH straight down until you reach about 5 ppm of CO_2. This will predict your new pH without CO_2 addition. You can clearly see from the graph that the pH swing will be most severe at low values of KH.

Summary

You may have to look through this chapter a few times. Don't worry: It will make sense and will actually help you in your tank keeping.

Part Three
Selecting Your Equipment

"MY planted aquarium was growing fine until the fish paid a neighborhood kid to come and mow"

Top Tanks and Stand-Up Stands

The single most important item to start your new hobby is an aquarium. They come in a wide variety of sizes, shapes, and materials. Let's talk about tank basics and help you decide which tank is best for you. You will also want something to put your tank on, so we will also talk about stands.

Glass Aquariums

Most aquariums are built from glass or acrylic. Each material has good and bad points. Glass is clear and is very hard to scratch. These aquariums are constructed of glass panels that are joined with silicone sealer. They also usually have a plastic frame that adds stability to the aquarium. The basic sizes for glass aquariums are:

Glass aquariums are very clear and offer resistance to scratches.

Chart of Popular Aquarium Sizes

Volume (Gallons)	Dimensions (Inches)	Weight Full (Pounds)
2 1/2 Mini Tank	12x6x8	27
5 1/2	16x8x10	62
10	20x10x12	111
15	24x12x12	170
15 High	20x10x18	170
20	24x12x16	225
20 Long	30x12x12	225
25	24x12x20	282
29	30x12x18	330
30	36x12x16	343
30 Breeder	36x18x12	343
33 Long	48x13x12	382
37	30x12x22	415
38	36x12x20	427
40 Breeder	36x18x16	458
40 Long	48x13x16	455
45	36x12x24	515
50	36x18x18	600
55	48x13x20	625
65	36x18x24	775
75	48x18x20	850
90	48x18x24	1050
120	48x24x24	1400
125	72x18x22	1400
150	72x18x28	1800
180	72x24x24	2100

Part 3

There are other shapes available to fit unique spaces or fill custom orders if you would like. Your local aquarium supply shop can guide you along in the special-order process.

Volume (Gallons)	Dimensions (Inches)	Comments
54 Corner	38x27x22	A three-sided tank
92 Corner	48x34x24	
26 Bow Front	24x15x21	A standard four-sided tank with a curved front
36 Bow Front	30x15x21	
46 Bow Front	36x15x20	
72 Bow Front	48x18x22	
155 Bow Front	72x24x24	
10 Hexagon	14x12x18	A six-sided tank
20 Hexagon	18x16x20	
35 Hexagon	23x20x24	
60 Hexagon	27x24x28	

A glass aquarium will meet the needs of most new aquarists. You can see that there will certainly be a size and shape that will fit your space, but glass tanks do have drawbacks. First, they can break. There is usually no good way to repair a broken aquarium. Small tanks can sometimes be sealed if there is a crack, but it will be noticeable. The cost of actually repairing the glass is nearly as much as buying a replacement; with time figured in, it's usually just not worth it. The larger the aquarium, the more potential there is for a disaster. Imagine 50 gallons or more of water all over the living room floor–ouch!

The second problem with glass aquariums, especially large ones, is the weight of the tank when empty. Small aquariums aren't much of a problem, but once you get much above a 55-gallon glass tank, it becomes very hard to move. A 55-gallon tank weighs nearly 80 pounds without water. A 120-gallon tank weighs 215 pounds. I like large tanks, but it takes too many people to move a glass tank.

The size as well as the shape of your aquarium is very important for proper plant growth.

Acrylic Aquariums

Acrylic is a very clear plastic material that is used for aquariums. The standard sizes will be the same found for glass aquariums. You will also find a wider variety of novelty shapes, like half cylinder, bubble, and tall columns, due to the greater strength and workability of the acrylic. You can just do a little more with this material. Acrylic is a more expensive material, so tanks made with acrylic will cost more.

Acrylic aquariums are much stronger because the panels are chemically bonded to each other. You can only stick glass together but not fuse it. Acrylic is also about half the weight of glass. I already said that I like large aquariums. I would definitely consider investing in an acrylic aquarium for tanks larger than 75 gallons. My husband and I can move my 240-gallon aquarium when it is empty. There is no way we could do that with a glass one.

The thing that probably prevents more people from buying acrylic is the cost. It also scratches more easily than glass. I own two acrylic aquariums, and yes, they both have scratches. You must be very careful cleaning the surface to avoid scratching it. My best advice is to let your budget and the size of the tank determine the material that you choose.

Tanks for Plants

Some sizes of aquariums are better suited to growing plants. Very tall tanks are a problem because it is difficult to get good light penetration to the plants lower in the tank. So you should usually pass on any tank called a "Tall," though they can be affective if you want a tank full of tall a Vallisneria and nothing else. Breeder-sized tanks are often a little shorter. For example, a 75-gallon tank has nearly the same dimensions as a 90-gallon tank. The 90-gallon tank is just 4 inches deeper. The 75-gallon tank is a better choice.

You will also notice that another way to add gallons to a tank is to just make it wider. The 75-gallon aquarium is the same length and height as a standard 55-gallon aquarium, but it is just 5 inches wider. A planted aquarium looks much better with this added width. So you will probably be happier with an aquarium that is wider and not too tall.

One final point to consider when purchasing your tank is the lighting. If you buy a complete setup, make sure that the hood can accommodate the brighter lights that a planted tank will require.

Stand Up for Stands

There are so many different types of aquarium stands that you should easily be able to find one that you like. What follows is a brief list of things to consider when selecting your stand:

• The stand should be of sturdy construction and be able to safely hold your aquarium. The bottom of the aquarium must be well supported and should touch the stand all around its edges and with several supports in the middle. Good support is especially critical for large aquariums. A large piece of glass or acrylic on the bottom of a tank can deform or break without adequate support.

• The stand should hold your equipment and conceal it in an attractive way. Some stands are open on the bottom, but this is not a problem, just not as pretty.

• The stand should be built so that it is level. The floor it is on at the store may not be level, so it may be hard to check.

There are many materials that stands are built from. Wood, laminates, and metal are all popular choices. Remember that whatever stand you decide to purchase, it will probably get wet once in a while. When doing tank maintenance, wipe up any drops to preserve the beauty of your stand.

Build Your Own

It is really not that difficult to build a stand for an aquarium. If you are handy with home projects, you can build your own and have something unique that may even cost less than a store-bought stand.

Be sure to have a solid stand for your aquarium.

Adequate support should be the basis for any home-built stand. A basic box built from two-by-fours makes a good core for a home-built stand. From there you can use nice wood or other materials to cover the box. You may need to use something more of a sturdy construction, like a four-by-four in a stand for a very large tank.

You can also find somebody to build a custom stand for you, if you want. Most suppliers of custom-made aquariums will also build custom stands.

Lighting for Planted Aquariums

Proper lighting will have a big impact on your success with your planted aquarium. As you already know, light is the key ingredient in the photosynthesis process of plants. The life of plants is 100 percent dependent on light.

Normally, the sun provides all the light that an aquatic plant needs. The amount of light that is required will depend on the type of plant. Most aquatic plants grow best where they have full sun for most of the day. There are also many plants that grow in and around water in shady areas. These will not need as much light to grow. All aquatic plants will grow faster and larger with proper lighting.

Providing proper lighting is the next step to success with planted tanks.

Too much light will promote unwanted algae growth.

Will more light help? It will, but only up to a point. When you grow aquatic plants in an aquarium, light, CO_2, and nutrients are all required in balance. If you have an excess of any of these three, the growth of the plants will be limited. So if you have really bright lights but no supplemental CO_2, the plants won't grow any faster and you are just paying more for your electric bill. With too much light you could promote algae growth, which is not attractive either.

How Much Light?

There are many ways to measure how much light a particular lamp is putting out. Most require purchasing a device to measure the output. I think this is overkill for the beginner. If you are really interested in light, there are many resources to learn more. Let's just give a few definitions so that you will be familiar with these terms.

Lumens

A lumen is the measure of light energy produced by a bulb. Light bulbs also give off energy as heat. Many bulb manufacturers will have the Lumen rating for their bulbs.

Lux

Lux is the amount of lumens per square meter. You can buy a luxmeter and measure the amount of light you are getting. This is not necessary at all unless you are really into lights.

Watts

Watts is the amount of power that is used by a lamp. It does not tell you how much of that energy is given off as light or heat. Watts is the easiest measure of lighting power for most aquarists to use. We will talk mostly about watts here.

Color Temperature (Degrees Kelvin)

Degrees Kelvin (K) is a measure of the color quality of the bulb. Natural daylight measures about 5500K while most incandescent bulbs measure around 2700K. The higher the Kelvin number, the more blue a light will look. 6500K has a pleasing appearance for most aquariums and is considered the "best" for planted aquaria.

The Following are Other Kelvin Ratings:

• 2700 or 27–orange shade common for compact fluorescent lamps, similar to many incandescent lamps.

• 3000 or 30–"warm white," similar to whiter shades of incandescent.

• 3500 or 35–between warm white and cool white, similar to the whitest halogen lamps and projector lamps.

• 4100 or 41–"cool white" or the color of average sunlight.

• 5000 or 50–an icy cold pure white like that of noontime tropical sunlight.

• 6500 or 65–slightly bluish white or "daylight."

The Watts Rule

The standard rule of thumb for planted aquariums is that you need 2 to 5 watts of light per gallon. For most of us, this is a perfectly acceptable way to choose lights for our aquariums. You can have a nice planted tank at the low light of 2 watts per gallon. Keep in mind that unless you are going to go "high tech," you will not need the higher light levels of 4 to 5 watts per gallon.

Actinic Light

As you shop for lighting, you will see the term actinic used in reference to aquarium lighting. Actinic is a very blue wavelength (above 10,000K), which is needed for the health of photosynthetic corals. Actinic lights are for reef tanks and not planted tanks.

Types of Lights

There are many types of lights available for use with aquariums. You may only see some of these types with old aquarium equipment. Let's review the lighting choices that you will find.

Incandescent Lights

These are the old familiar light bulbs. They are very inefficient. They give off more heat than light. You will probably not find this type of bulb in new equipment. My advice is to not use them. It is a waste of electricity for a fish tank.

Part 3

The use of waterproof endcaps is always recommended, especially over open aquariums.

Metal Halide Lights

Metal halide lighting is especially popular with reef aquarist. It provides a very intense light, so it is good for deep aquariums. Metal halide lamps commonly have a 5500K or 6500K color rating, which is very good for aquariums with plants. These lamps also have a high wattage rating. The smallest commonly found is a 150-watt bulb.

Metal halide lamps have several drawbacks for aquarium use. The bulb should be at least 6 inches from the top of the tank. They are also very hot bulbs. A cooling fan installed into the hood of the tank will be needed to prevent overheating. Your water can be overheated by the bulb as well, something to keep an eye on if you use them. Finally, they are expensive compared with other types of lighting.

Perhaps the best use of a metal halide lamp for a planted tank is as a spot light over a certain region of your tank. You can then choose plants with higher lighting requirements to inhabit that area.

Standard Fluorescent Lights

Fluorescent lamps come in all shapes and sizes, but they all work on the same basic principle: An electric current stimulates mercury atoms, which causes them to release ultraviolet photons. Your lamp will have a small amount of mercury inside the tube. These photons in turn stimulate a phosphor, which emits visible light photons. The phosphor used is a coating on the inside of the tube. The type of phosphor used will affect the color temperature (degrees Kelvin) of the light produced. Fluorescent lamps are two to four times more efficient than incandescent lamps. They produce more light for the energy used.

As with metal halide bulbs, fluorescent lamps require ballasts for proper operation. The ballast provides a controlled flow of electricity to the fluorescent tube that it requires for operation. Quick-start ballasts fire up the lamp faster and are commonly used. Electronic ballasts are a little more expensive but they are smaller, which adds some benefits to fitting the lamps in a smaller hood.

How to Read a Fluorescent Tube

A standard tube will have a number on it that is a standard identifier for the industry. Here is a key so that you can read your tube.

Example: F30T12/CW/RS

"F" = fluorescent.

"30" = rated nominal wattage.

"T" = indicates shape; this lamp is shaped like a tube.

"12" = diameter in eighths of an inch; this lamp is 12/8 (1.5) inches in diameter.

"CW" = color; this lamp is a cool white lamp. You may also see a number here like 741. This would indicate a 4100K tube.

"RS" = mode of starting; the lamp is a rapid-start lamp. Preheat lamps do not have "RS" as a suffix. HO or VHO in this position indicates a "High Output" or "Very High Output" tube respectively.

The standard fluorescent light will work well for planted aquariums. They are especially useful for low-light-level tanks. They can be extremely economical also. You can grow very nice plants under inexpensive shop lights found in home improvement stores. Just remember to use a good daylight or grow bulb.

HO and VHO Fluorescent Lights

HO is an abbreviation of "High Output" and VHO stands for "Very High Output." These bulbs will put out more light than a standard fluorescent. They also require different ballasts. For example, compared with a standard 48-inch T12 standard bulb (40 watts), an HO will give you 60 watts and a VHO gives 115 watts. The advantage is tremendous when it comes to saving space in your hood. You get the output of almost three normal tubes from one VHO tube.

There are some downsides. The tubes are more expensive and will not last as long. A VHO

Part 3

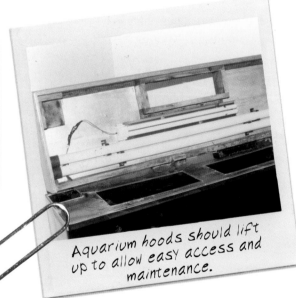

Fluorescent tubes should be replaced to maintain the proper level of light for your tank. They may come on, but the quality of the light degrades over time.

Aquarium hoods should lift up to allow easy access and maintenance.

tube should be replaced every four to five months. A normal fluorescent tube should be changed every year.

Compact Fluorescent Lights

Relatively new to the aquarium market, power compact fluorescent lights are often the light of choice for many aquarists. The lamp will have two tubes that are a smaller diameter than standard T12 fluorescents. A 33-inch bulb puts out 96 watts of light. Getting pretty close to our VHOs! Another bonus is that the lamp will often last 14 to 16 months. Is this the best light for planted aquariums? I think for the price, compact size, and life of the bulb, it is nearly ideal.

Aquarium Hoods

After you have chosen your light source, you will need a hood or other fixture to hold it above your aquarium. My best advice is to look around and see what you like. Many are simply wooden boxes that sit above the aquarium and contains the lights. As we already mentioned, some of these lamps can be quite hot. Hoods with cooling fans are an option and are often very common for reef aquariums that use the higher output lights.

Many companies make hoods or canopies that are designed to fit over your aquarium where you can select the type of lights included.

Finally, the common strip light that comes with many aquarium packages will probably not be adequate for your planted aquarium. There is a very cool solution for you out there! Several companies have come out with a power compact fluorescent kit that will fit into a standard strip light. They are very economical but require you to do the work yourself.

Filtration Equipment

Many debate whether you need to run a filter for a well-planted aquarium. It is possible to go without if you are very diligent with changing your water. I think that a good filter will benefit most tanks. You can weigh the options, but let's assume that you want to acquire a filter for your tank.

Filters perform several jobs. First is the removal of solid waste. Most filters will have a fibrous bag or use filter floss to trap large particles. You will need to clean them periodically to keep your tank healthy but eventually they will wear out and need to be replaced.

Second, filters can be used to contain materials

Having the proper filtration is a necessity for good plant growth over extended periods.

that will change the chemistry of the water in your aquarium. Activated carbon is a common material to place in the filter box. It will remove organic materials and can remove odors from your tank. Once the carbon is used up, you will need to replace it with new material. I don't use it on a planted tank unless there is a big problem with brown water. My preference is to use frequent water changes to solve any water chemistry problems.

Finally, your aquarium filter can work as a biological filter. A good aquarium filter will provide plenty of surface area for the "good guy" bacteria. A well-planted tank doesn't accumulate as much ammonia from fish waste as one without plants, and biological filter is generally not considered to be as important for a well-planted tank. Taking all of these factors into account, solids removal is the most important job for a filter used on your planted aquarium. Not all filters make good solid-removal devices. Let's talk about those which will do a good job of removing some of the solids.

Power Filters

These are the filters that hang on the back of aquariums. This design has been around for a very long time. Improvements in the layout and filter materials have made this filter type a little more convenient than the old days. Most will be able to prime themselves. The older styles required you to start the siphon yourself. I still use filters like this and it is a real treat to suck up fish water to get them started after each cleaning.

The design is very simple. A long tube will hang down into the aquarium to suck up the dirty water. Solids are trapped in filter bags of floss and clean water is returned to the tank. The flow of water going back to the tank is usually fast enough to create a nice current that directs the solids to the intake tube.

The filter box can also hold activated carbon for chemical filtration. The filter bag will also act as a biological filter, if you use the same one for several months. You can just rinse the baggie or filter mat in cold water to remove the solids that have built up. The good bacteria will be happy to live on the filter material.

How to Choose a Power Filter?

Most pet stores will sell power filters. There are several well-known brands. People usually develop preferences for certain brands. It is often just a matter of personal choice. Look around, ask questions, and decide which type of filter is right for you.

You should choose the size filter that is rated for your tank. The manufacturer will publish the flow rate for the particular filter and list the size tank that it fits. A good rule of thumb is to look for a filter that has a flow rate of three to five times the tank volume. If you have a 30-gallon tank, look for a filter that has a flow rate of 90 to 150 gallons per hour. You may have to buy two filters to get the desired filtration rate if your tank is large.

Bio wheels add a lot of surface area to conventional filters.

Bio Wheels

A bio wheel is a device added to some power filters that provides lots of surface area for bacterial growth. They look like a water wheel at the top of the filter. Bio wheels work well and are no problem with a well-planted aquarium.

Canister Filters

Canister filters sit below your aquarium and consist of a motor unit and container to hold the filtration media. The tubes will run down the back of the tank to the filter. They will not operate well unless they are below the tank as they rely on gravity to help water flow into the canister.

Inside the canister you will usually find baskets that will hold activated carbon or other treatment materials. There will also be a basket that holds some sort of material that will encourage the growth of nitrogen cycle bacteria. Most also hold some sort of sponge or fibrous material for trapping solids.

Most are well designed to allow easy removal of the tubes without spilling so that you can clean the filter. They may not require cleaning as frequently as a power filter. It's still best not to let them go too long between cleanings, because the accumulated mulm can begin to decay. I usually clean out my canister every month and power filters every two weeks.

Wet/dry filters often have biotowers similar to this one.

How to Choose a Canister Filter

Choosing a canister filter is similar to choosing a power filter. Check the flow rate of the filter unit and match it to the size of your tank. As always, ask around, do some research, and choose the filter that will best meet your particular needs.

Other Types of Filters

There are many other types of filters available. My advice is to buy a power filter or a canister filter. Let's just look at some of the other types and rate the pros and cons:

Wet/Dry Filters

These were originally designed for use with marine aquariums. They are primarily biological filters and will feature "bio balls" or some other high-surface area material. They really aren't needed for a well-planted aquarium. It was originally thought that they were detrimental since it was believed that they removed too much carbon dioxide from the water. It has been found that they really aren't a problem for CO_2 but they have no benefit for the planted tank either.

Fluidized Bed

These are also a type of biological filter that uses sand as the "surface area." Water is pumped into the sand bed to agitate the sand and keep all of the particles moving. I like these for tanks with fish only. Again, your needs for biological filtration don't require this type of filter for a planted aquarium.

Diatomaceous Earth Filters

These filters use a slurry of diatomaceous earth to make a cake that can filter out very fine particles. They are best used as a "polishing" filter to clean up a problem in the water like an algae bloom. Since there are probably better ways to deal with most problems, they aren't a necessary item.

Part 3

Carbon Dioxide Equipment

If you have not yet reviewed Chapter 6, you may want to go back and take a peek. I will assume that you are pretty familiar with why CO_2 is beneficial to a planted aquarium. I will also assume that you are at least a little familiar with how CO_2 can affect your water chemistry.

CO_2 equipment for your tank can be very simple and inexpensive or complex and relatively expensive. Let's begin with the simple and finish up this chapter with the more complex.

I think I should mention here that you do not need to use supplemental carbon dioxide at all. It is very possible to grow a nice planted tank

The use of carbon dioxide is considered a must in today's modern planted tanks.

without. You may also decide to add it later as you become familiar with growing plants in the aquarium. Your plants will grow faster with CO_2 addition and in the long run, you may like the results more.

Make Me Gassy

Many people take advantage of a natural fermentation process to provide carbon dioxide gas for their planted aquarium. Yeast, used for bread making or brewing, uses sugar and produces ethanol and CO_2 gas for its life cycle. Humans have taken advantage of this process since ancient times. Wine was first produced in Mesopotamia around 6,000 B.C. The Egyptians began making the first yeast-leavened breads around 3,000 B.C. Glad the ancients had their priorities straight and got wine figured out first.

The point is that the yeasts used for these crafts have had thousands of years to "evolve" for their jobs. Bread yeasts generally produce more CO_2 than alcohol, wine yeasts do the opposite. That makes sense. So which type of yeast should an aquatic gardener use? At first glance, good bakers (bread) yeast should work well. Fermenting with baker's yeast will produce lots of CO_2 quickly but bread yeasts don't like much alcohol and will poison themselves at about 10 percent alcohol. So for a longer, more-sustained fermentation try good wine yeast. They can handle higher alcohol content, up to 18 percent ethanol. My advice is to go ahead and use baker's yeast but when you get the hang of it, why not try brewing yeast? You could turn this whole thing into your own little science project.

Brew Recipe

You can use table sugar as the base ingredient for your brew. Two pounds of sugar dissolved in up to a gallon of liquid gives a good concentration of sugar for a long fermentation. A gallon of liquid is quite a lot, so just adjust the recipe as needed. There's a little trick to dissolving the sugar. You want to end up with a gallon total of liquid–don't add a gallon of water to the sugar or you will have more than a gallon. Put your sugar in the container first, and then fill it to the desired amount. I don't worry about any solid sugar that remains on the bottom, as the yeast "eat" the dissolved sugar thus the solid will go into solution.

Yeast uses sugar and produces ethanol and CO_2 gas for its life cycle.

Yeasts also need other nutrients for growth besides sugar. You can try adding a little frozen fruit juice or molasses in your mix. Home-brew

Part 3

outfits also sell some additives to feed yeast that contain minerals and vitamins. I have also read that a half of a multivitamin pill in the mix (gallon) is also good for them. No problem experimenting a little with your mix. The goal is to get a good long fermentation. Please don't drink your brew! Other bacteria than yeast can and will live in your mix. The yeast will out compete most of them but there are probably enough "bad guys" growing in there to give you a good bellyache. And there's no problem pouring your spent brew down the drain, it's all organic.

Fermentation Equipment

There is one commercially available fermentation-based product on the market for aquarium use. I use it and like it very much. It is small but practical. I get about one to two weeks of CO_2 production from it. If you want to get serious about using fermented sugar for CO_2 production, you may want to check out a home-brewing catalog or store. In general, the larger the container that you use, the more CO_2 will be produced. The length of the fermentation will depend on the temperature, the sugar concentration of the started solution and other chemical properties that you can't control. Most home-brew kits are based on a large 5-gallon container (called a carboy). Look for a smaller carboy if you can unless you have a large aquarium. The more liquid you ferment the more gas you will produce.

The second part of the problem is delivering the gas to your aquarium. The trick is to somehow mix the gas with the water in a way that encourages the most gas to dissolve in the water. Strange concept that gas actually is "dissolved" in water, but that's exactly what happens. You want to mix the CO_2 that you have produced with the water very well. A "diffuser" or "reactor" is a piece of equipment designed just for that purpose. There are many designs out there and they all probably work fine, especially for a fermentation system. Most good local aquarium retailers will have what you need.

DIY Home Brew

You can easily build your own home fermenter. All it takes is a container that can be closed, tubing, and a tight lid. I will warn you; there are some real ugly stories out there about people building up pressure in their home systems and blowing fermenter goop all over the walls! Smells like bread. A very popular design is to use a 1-liter soda bottle. Go ahead and try your own design if you like. But have a mop ready just in case.

The diffuser will allow good mixing of the carbon dioxide and the tank's water.

To prevent blow outs, make sure that the gas can escape from the fermenter at all times. Make sure that there is nothing blocking or stopping the flow of gas. The bottle could build up pressure that will lead to the type of blow out mentioned previously. It is like shaking up a bottle of soda and opening it–all that pressure and gas needs to go somewhere.

I'll Take My Gas in a Can

You can easily get started with CO_2 addition with a fermentation system or you can go right to using a pressurized gas system. The upfront cost is much larger but there is much less work involved. You will have a ready supply of CO_2–no messing around with witches brew.

The very first thing I need to do is warn you about working with compressed gas in cylinders. They can be very dangerous. I have worked in many labs where many types of gases were used. Proper handling and use of compressed gases was a big part of our training. I know people who have been badly injured and I know of one person killed due to carelessness with compressed gas. When you handle your compressed gas equipment responsibly, it is very safe. But like a snake, it will bite you if you don't play nice.

Safety First

Here is a list of the most important safety considerations for handling compressed CO_2 cylinders.

Do not drop cylinders or permit them to strike anything violently. If you knock the top valve from a cylinder, it becomes a jet propelled rocket that can strike you. The amount of gas released may also be a problem in a closed space. You will suffocate in a room full of CO_2. If a cylinder is tied down, but discharging uncontrollably, open a window and leave the room until it has completely discharged. CO_2 is heavier than air, so it will build up from the ground to the ceiling. Just like dry ice fog (dry ice is solid CO_2), it hugs the ground.

The large metal cap on top of a new cylinder is used for valve protection. It should be kept on the cylinder at all times except when the cylinder is actually being used or charged. Cylinders should not be transported without safety caps. A cylinder's cap should be screwed all the way down on the cylinder's neck ring and should fit securely. Do not lift cylinders by the cap. The cap is for valve protection to prevent the violent discharge of gas described above.

Open cylinder valves *SLOWLY.* Do not use a wrench to open or close a hand wheel-type cylinder valve. If it cannot be operated by hand, the valve should be repaired. Your compressed-gas supplier can repair your cylinder or offer you a replacement. It's not worth saving a little money by messing around with a compressed-gas cylinder.

Do not attempt to repair cylinder valves or their relief devices while a cylinder contains gas pressure.

Always use the proper regulator for the gas in the cylinder and always check the regulator before attaching it to a cylinder. If the connections do not fit together readily, the wrong regulator is being used.

The threads and mating surfaces of the regulator and hose connections should be cleaned before the regulator is attached. Always use a cylinder wrench or another tightly fitting wrench to tighten the regulator nut and hose connections. Attach the regulator securely before opening the valve wide. Finally, stand to the side of the regulator when opening the cylinder valve. Don't let the compressed gas impact your body.

DO NOT transport your tank inside your car. Always put the cylinder in the trunk. If the tank becomes damaged or the safety valve pops, you could find yourself in a car full of CO_2. It may be enough to cause you to pass out behind the wheel! Aquarists have actually had this happen to them (had cylinders discharge inside the car)–please be very careful.

Equipment You Will Need
You will need the following equipment to complete a compressed CO_2 system for your tank.

Gas Cylinder
You will be able to purchase you gas cylinder and get it refilled at most local welding-

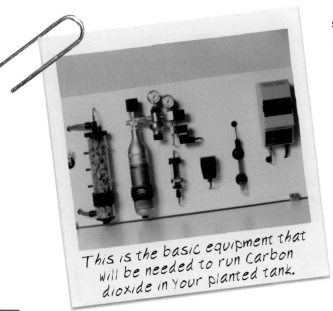

This is the basic equipment that will be needed to run Carbon dioxide in your planted tank.

supply outlets. A 5-pound tank will be about the right size. There is no problem going with a smaller tank. Pick one that fits well underneath your stand. They aren't very pretty.

Regulator

The regulator is a device that you must have. It attaches to the main outlet of the cylinder and let's you control the flow of gas from the cylinder. You will not be able to control your gas without one. Your regulator should be designed for use with CO_2.

Check Valve

A check valve is a one-way valve. It protects your regulator from water coming back from your tank.

Bubble Counter

You can purchase or build a bubble counter. The bubble counter is what you will use to measure the amount of gas going into your system.

Diffuser/Reactor

The reactor will ensure good mixing of the CO_2 gas with your tank water.

CO_2 Resistant Tubing

PVC tubing will be resistant to the CO_2 gas. Tubing should only be used on the low-pressure side of your system, after the regulator. Other tubing can actually leak CO_2 through the walls of the tubing.

Needle Valve

A needle valve is a type of valve that gives you very fine control of your gas. You don't necessarily need one, but it will make controlling your gas flow much easier. They are expensive but probably worth the extra cash.

In a basic set up, the equipment above will be assembled in the order listed above. Take a look at the drawing to get a look at the proper lay out.

Give Me Control

You can take your compressed-gas system a step forward where you add a pH controller and solenoid valve. This will give you very hands-off, well-controlled system. I will warn you that you will need to spend some cash for a good system.

pH Controller

This is a device that will measure the pH in your tank periodically (nearly continuously) and then control an automatic valve to the CO_2 system. Remember that CO_2 makes the pH of your tank go down. When the pH goes up to a certain point, the controller will open the CO_2 valve and allow the gas to flow until the pH is back to the control point. How cool is that!

Your pH controller will require monthly calibration. You will use a test solution with a known pH (called a standard solution) and make sure that your controller measures the same pH as the solution.

Solenoid Valve

This is the automatic valve that your controller opens. Make sure that the control valve will work with your particular controller. It is easiest to buy them as a pair. Many manufacturers will supply a controller/valve combo. I also want you to look for a valve that fails CLOSED. If there is a power failure or problem you want the valve to stay closed. If it fails OPEN, all of your gas will leak out and you may poison your fish with too much CO_2. Yes, you can kill all the fish with too much.

Putting It All Together

If you are willing to spend the money, you can purchase your complete system from one supplier. Many aquarium suppliers offer complete systems. There are some advantages to going this way. The manufacturer has probably mated the parts and tested the system for aquarium application. This can reduce your time tinkering with the system. The downside is that you may pay more for a complete system compared with shopping for best prices on the individual parts. Follow the manufacturer's directions for assembly.

Leak Check

Attach all tubing and components carefully to eliminate leaks. Use CO_2 resistant Teflon tape to protect and help seal any threaded fittings. Use hose clamps on the tubing that has hose barb connections.

Secure Your Cylinder

Take the extra time to find a way to strap your tank securely to its final resting place. You may need to modify your stand. It can be as simple as adding a couple of holes to run a strap through. The cylinder should be stored standing up with the regulator on top. Laying it on its side can potentially damage the regulator.

Start Your System

Now slowly open all the valves. Make sure that the regulator is closed and slowly open the cylinder main valve. You will see the pressure gauges on the regulator go up. Next open the regulator until the outlet pressure gauge reads 20 psi (this opens the check valve; psi means pounds per square inch). Now back off the pressure to about 12 to 15 psi. You should be getting a bubble of gas every few seconds.

If you are using a needle valve, keep the regulator pressure at 20 psi. Now open and slowly adjust the needle valve until you see the bubble count that you want. Add the CO_2 slowly and monitor your tank. You can shut off the gas at night to be safe until you know what level of gas you want to add.

You can monitor the pH of your tank until you reach the desired target pH. If you use a controller, it will do the job for you but testing never hurts. Remember to check and double check all of your equipment often to make sure that it's working properly.

Other Equipment to Consider

We have hit the big three equipment purchases for your planted tank–lights, filters, and CO_2 equipment. Let's move on to some other items that you will need or may find useful. Over time, if you are like most aquarist, you will end up with a collection of gadgets.

Putting the Heat On

The fish you will be keeping will probably be tropical species. They will require water that is 68 to 82 degrees Fahrenheit. Depending on your climate, you may need to heat your water. There is a wide variety of aquarium heaters on the market. They are inexpensive and most brands work pretty well. You will need about 5 watts of heating per gallon of water. Aquarium heaters come in sizes from 50

Warm water is required for lush plant growth.

Fishes as well as plants will benefit from a temperature-controlled environment.

Always use a thermometer in your aquarium.

to 200 watts. Many people feel that it is better to use several smaller heaters rather than one large heater. If it should "fail on," the small heater will probably not cook your fish. If the heater "fails off," the tank will have a back up so that it won't get too cold.

You will find heaters that hang on the tank or are completely submersible. Either type will work well, let your personal preference guide your choice. Many heaters will have a dial that lets you set the temperature. Others will only have a dial to increase the temperature. I strongly recommend that you keep a thermometer in your tank to monitor the temperature with either type of heater. Slowly adjust your heater until it is keeping your tank at the desired temperature.

Substrate Heating

The Dutch method of building a planted aquarium advocates the use of substrate heating. The theory is that heating cables placed in the gravel bed create water currents that help move nutrients to the roots. It has also been suggested that it helps the development of beneficial bacteria in the gravel bed as well. Takashi Amano has also used substrate heating by placing a heating pad underneath the bottom glass.

Some people swear by substrate heating, but it is not a necessity. If you decide to try a substrate heater, you will be able to purchase kits for aquarium use. They are fairly expensive. Look for a system that has very low wattage. For a heating pad, there are several brands of heating mats for aquariums sold for keeping reptiles. Adding a rheostat will let you control the amount of heat the mat puts out. Substrate heating will not replace a conventional aquarium heater, you will still need one.

Water Change Helpers

Frequent partial water changes will be the single best thing you can do for your aquarium. The best way to keep a healthy tank to make sure that your water is very clean. The best way to do this is by changing the water. Out with the old and in with the new. Planted tanks also benefit from a regular schedule of water changes.

There are several brands of water changer/gravel vacuums on the market that will make your life so much easier. Go buy one! They hook up to your faucet and let you suck up debris from the bottom of the tank while removing water. You simply go back to the sink and switch the adapter to refill your tank. I couldn't live without mine.

Bring Me My Bucket

Buckets can come in very handy for many uses. You can do water changes with them. You can place fish in them temporarily. They are great for holding your plants and keeping them wet while you arrange the tank. You can carry rocks in them. You need to have at least one good bucket!

Test Kits

Another must have. You need good-quality test kits for pH, KH, dGH, ammonia, nitrite, and nitrate. If you are going to use CO_2 you must know the pH and hardness parameters of your aquarium. You may be able to find a large test kit that will have many of these tests in one package. Don't skimp on your test kits, they are very important.

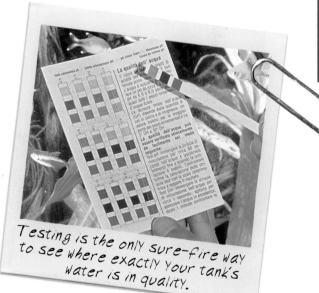

Testing is the only sure-fire way to see where exactly your tank's water is in quality.

Odds and Ends

I am sure that you will acquire many tools and toys as you move forward with your tank. Here is a list of some of the items that you will probably need sooner rather than later.

Part 3

Real wood can darken the tank's water.

Artificial wood often looks like the real thing.

Nets–It's best to have more than one and a couple of different sizes. My favorite way to catch a fish is to place a large net on one end of the tank and use the small one to chase the fish into the big net. It's a good idea to clean your nets after each use. Wash them well in hot water.

Algae Scrub Pad–Make sure that whatever you use is designed for use with your aquarium. Acrylic will scratch very easily and you cannot use the same algae scrubber that can be used with a glass tank. The side of a plastic credit card works really well as a scraper. On a glass tank, you can carefully scrape algae with a razor blade–don't try it with acrylic!

Planting Tools–And finally many people like to use planting tools. If you don't like to use your fingers for planting and trimming, small scissors, hemostats, tweezers, and chopsticks are just some of the tools used to assist in planting and trimming your tank.

Fish Food–Don't forget to buy some good-quality foods for your new fish. Flakes and pellets are fine for most fish. There are also many frozen foods available that make a good treat for your fish. Most fish foods will tell you which kind of fish you can feed with their diet. Live foods are also sometimes available or you can grow your own.

Water Conditioners–If you will be using city water, you will probably need a good dechlorinator. Add the dechlorinator each time you do a water change. Let's say you are doing a 20 percent water change on your 50-gallon tank. You would not add the dose for the whole 50 gallons of water, just for the 20 percent (10 gallons) that you took out.

Bogwood comes in many shapes and sizes.

Lava rocks are used to create a realistic landscape.

Other water chemicals to consider are baking soda (to raise the KH) and calcium carbonate (raises dGH and KH). Be careful with any pH up or down chemicals. They may contain phosphates. Phosphates can aggravate an algae bloom in your tank so always try to use phosphate-free additives.

Plant Nutrients–Look for some fertilizer tabs that go into the gravel and a good liquid formula that has trace elements. There are several excellent products on the market. We will talk about using these later.

Decorations–Rocks and driftwood are traditional decorations used in planted aquariums. Rocks should be non calciferous. They should not contain calcium compounds in them. This type of rock will change your water chemistry, making the dGH and KH go up. Avoid limestone, sandstone, and tufa rock. Granite, slate, quartz, petrified wood, and lava rock should be fine for your tank.

Not all types of wood make good tank driftwood. The wood should be hard and attractive. If you live near a beach, you can look for real driftwood. Many aquarium stores also sell driftwood. You may need to soak your wood for quite awhile before adding it to your tank. Mopani wood, which is popular in the trade, will leach some tannins for awhile. The brown color in your water from these tannins is not bad, but not pretty either. Soaking your wood in a bucket and changing the water will prepare it for your tank.

Of course you can't forget to add a plastic sand castle, bubbling diver, or pirate treasure chest to your tank for that special touch!

Part Four

Putting It All Together

"You planted what?"

Start Your Engines

You are now armed with the information that you will need to plan and build your planted aquarium. What to do? How do you get started? I think that you will get the best result by planning your layout. What plants do you want to keep? What style? Where will you place the plants in the tank?

The first thing to do is consider the size of your tank. If it is small, you may want to concentrate on only a few different plants. Too many different species crowded into a small space will look cluttered and uncoordinated. A large tank can certainly hold many more varieties of plants, but the design will not look coherent if they are not planted in a way that makes artistic sense. That is

Diversity comes in time. For now, concentrate on just a few types of plants.

Similar plants in different sizes provide contrasts.

where design becomes a personal matter. You can look at other designs and maybe even copy something you like. The true test is to develop your own style.

A good way to begin is to get out some paper, a set of colored pencils, and try some sketches. You don't have to be a great artist. Aquatic plants have a pretty broad range of colors and textures. You could just draw areas of color and texture to get a feel for how it might look. There are no hard-and-fast rules but here are some points to consider.

Tall in Back/Short in Front–That is pretty self-explanatory. Place the tallest plants in the back where they won't over-power smaller plants, which look good in the foreground.

Many Greens–There are many different shades of green. Use that to create an interesting aquascape.

Reds Stand Out–Just like a red traffic light, red plants command attention. You can overdo red. Don't forget that red plants also need more light.

Something Interesting–A single object that is unusual can help solidify your design. An interesting rock or several, great piece of driftwood, or an unusual plant can be used as a focal point in the tank.

On the Beach–A beach or area of a differently colored substrate can make an interesting statement in your tank.

Think 3-Dimensions–Your tank has an "up" direction as well as front to back. Think about different ways to use the depth of the tank.

Be Prepared

Now is the time to prepare your shopping list. First, buy all of the hardware that you need. We have gone over what you will need in great detail. You will probably get your equipment from a few different places, so it will probably not arrive all at the same time. No problem if you decide to add something, but make sure you have the big items lined up: tank, lights, filter, and a carbon dioxide dosing (CO_2) system (if you are going to use one).

I think it is a good idea to assemble all of the hardware for your tank before you buy any plants or animals. You can prepare your list of plants and animals ahead of time. You may need to plan ahead especially if you are ordering some special plants.

Substrates That Rate

We have not talked about a very important component of your planted aquarium yet–the substrate that you will use to grow your plants in. The planted aquarium hobby has really been growing since the early 1990s. You will really benefit from that fact. Ten years ago, you would have been experimenting with other dedicated hobbyists to find a good mix for growing your aquatic plants. There are now several brands of ready-to-use gravel substrate for the planted aquarium. As expected, they can be a little expensive, but they do work well and will give you good results.

Here are some alternatives, if you would like to save money and experiment a little.

Gravel and Laterite–Laterite is a clay-like soil that is mined from once-tropical areas. It is a rusty red color and is a fairly fine powder. Laterite contains iron that can be used by the roots of aquatic plants. Iron is an essential nutrient for good plant growth.

The typical way to use laterite is to add 1 inch of small gravel to the tank then add a layer of laterite, followed by another 2 to 3 inches of gravel. You will see this type of substrate talked about in the "Dutch Method." You can also buy balls of laterite that can be pushed down into the gravel of a tank that is already up and running. Laterite is a good additive to your substrate.

If you do not use a commercial plant-specific substrate, plan on using laterite in your substrate. About 1 pound of laterite is enough for a 55-gallon tank set up. The only down side to using laterite is that it is a very fine powder. If it is disturbed in your tank, it can create a cloudy mess.

Part 4

Gravel–Using gravel is fine unless the particle size is too small or too large. Gravel with too small of a particle size will not allow good transportation of nutrients. If it is too large, the nutrients won't be held into the gravel where you need it. Look for gravel that is 1/16th to 1/8th of an inch in diameter.

Sand–There are many, many types of sand that people have tried. Play sand and different types of blasting sands have all been tried. The results can be all right but a larger gravel will work better. Some of the big problems with sand is that any mulm that accumulates in the aquarium will sit on top of the sand and can look messy. It also tends to fly all over while your doing water changes, again making a big cloudy mess. My advice is to pass on the sand.

Peat Moss–Sphagnum peat moss is the material that accumulates in the bottom of sphagnum bogs. Peat moss is a common material used in gardening and is found in most commercial potting soils. Peat will lower the pH of your tank. It is an interesting material to work with in your tank and is probably best used if you are keeping fish that require a low pH environment. The problem with peat is that it likes to float and it can stain the water brown. If you decide to use it in your substrate, soak it for several days, and add it in a thin layer along with your laterite. Bury it well in 2 to 3 inches of gravel.

Blue gravel may not be the right choice for a natural look.

Bad Ideas–You may hear of all sorts of ideas for substrates. Some include things like kitty litter, manure, clay soils, and other common items. Save these "experiments" for the experts. You should avoid them unless your ready to break your tank down to remove whatever nasty gunk could result. The potential problem for many of these materials is that as they decompose they release sulfur dioxide gas. Sulfur dioxide is a product of anaerobic (without oxygen) decomposition of organic materials. This gas smells like rotten eggs and it can kill your fish.

Gravel Rules

Nothing is a bigger pain than after having gotten all your goodies together, you start setting up your tank and you don't have enough gravel. Here is a pretty easy way to figure out how much gravel to buy. First you will want a gravel bed that is at least 2 inches deep–3 inches is even better. To calculate the amount of gravel to buy, multiply the length by the width of the bottom of the tank. Then take this number and divide by 10. The result is the pounds of gravel that you will need for about a 2-inch depth. So if you want 3 inches, add half of the width multiplied by the length again to get the total.

Here is an example: **Q**–How much gravel should I buy for my 55-gallon aquarium for a 3-inch deep substrate bed? **A**–55-gallon aquariums have a footprint of 48 inches long and 13 inches wide. Forty-eight times 13 is 624 and half of that is 312. Adding the two numbers, I get 936, now dividing that by 10, I get about 94. So I should buy about 94 pounds of gravel.

Be sure to rinse your aquarium's gravel thoroughly.

Substrate Colors

You will be amazed at the colors of gravel you can find at your local pet-supply place. Neon orange, pink, green! It's enough to give a fish a heart attack! The reality is that fish do respond to the color of the substrate in their tank. It has been found that fish are more relaxed and display the best colors on dark neutral colors. That's great because those are also good colors for showing off your plants. Look for black, dark gray, browns, and even earthy reds. Let your plants and fish put on the show, not your gravel.

Use caution with gravel since some types may affect the tank's water chemistry.

Part 4

Your choice of background will have a dramatic effect on the tank's overall look.

Part 4

Some hobbyists choose to use stacked rocks behind their plants for a very natural look.

Backgrounds

Many aquariums, especially acrylic tanks, can be purchased with a blue or black background. Black and blue are attractive colors that will show off the colors of your fish well. I prefer the black with a planted tank. I think the blue would clash with all the different colors of the plants. Black actually can highlight many of the subtle reds and greens of your plants.

What if you want something different? What if plain blue or black is just too ho-hum? You can get very creative and make your tank unique. Use your imagination, but remember that your background will be competing with your plants.

Rocks can be glued to the back glass using aquarium-grade silicone caulk. Slate can be used to give a flat, dark gray background by applying flat pieces. You can try other types of rocks and build in little nooks for attaching plants or as caves for your fish. Lava rock is light weight, has an interesting texture, and is pretty inexpensive. Lava rock can usually be found in a red or black color. Just remember that if you glue rocks to the back, you will need to break down the whole tank to make changes.

Sheets of cork are also an interesting material that you can use. Look for the most "natural" product that you can. Avoid things that already have adhesives on the back or varnished on the surface. Art and craft stores usually have materials that are fairly free of additives. If you decide to use cork, I recommend soaking it in a bucket for awhile. Change the water in the bucket several times. Anything in the cork that might leach out will probably be gone after several water changes.

Another cool way to make a background is to make a moss wall. You can find a plastic mesh used for needle work at most craft stores. You use this mesh as a scaffolding for one of the aquatic mosses (Java moss or Christmas tree moss). You then attach the plastic mesh to the back of your tank—suction cups would be a great way. Then sit back and watch the moss fill out the bare spots.

Construction Zone

You have all the parts together, so now it's time to set up your tank. Let's go through the steps together. First is to pick a nice location for the aquarium. Most places will be fine. If you are placing the aquarium on a carpet, you may need to be careful that it is well balanced and has a solid footing. Metal stands are fine but probably not as sturdy as some wooden stands. You can consider discreetly bolting it to the wall with a small cable. Make sure that you find a stud in the wall for attachment. Another thing to consider with metal stands and carpets is that a tiny bit of water at the base of your stand can make a permanent rust stain on your carpet. Some sort of carpet protector may be in order.

Be sure your beautiful work of art is sitting on a sturdy base.

Strength and aesthetics are two qualities that aquarium stands should have.

You may also wish to avoid a place where the aquarium will receive a lot of natural light, from a window for example. But you are growing plants so wouldn't that be a good idea? Not really. First, sunlight is warm and can overheat your plants, if there is too much it can even cook your plants and fish. Second, tanks that have exposure to natural sunlight may be more prone to algae problems. You will not be able to control the amount of light that your tank will get and controlling the light is one way to control algae. This is a difficult issue since your plants could also benefit from the sunlight, but to play it safe, avoid direct sunlight.

Most aquarium stands are open in the back to give you easy access to the back of the aquarium. This lets you direct tubing from filters and electrical cords behind the aquarium. Before you get the tank in place, you may want to run any electrical connections that you may need under the tank. Extension cords or power strips may be needed to be placed. You will probably have several items that will require an electrical hookup; it's best to prepare ahead to avoid problems later.

Stand and Deliver

Now that you have the perfect place picked out, let's place your stand. First let me warn you. Don't expect to put the stand close to its eventual spot expecting to move it once the tank is in place. First it will be really heavy, even a small tank is surprisingly hefty. You better be Charles Atlas if you think you can move it at all once it is full of water. Even if you could do it, there is a chance of knocking the aquarium off the stand, breaking it, and flooding the room.

Place your stand on the floor in its new home. Leave room behind it for tubes or for your filter. You can use a ruler to measure a couple of inches away from the wall on both ends so that it is even. Now take out a level and check all of the sides. Adjust the heights of the corners until the stand is level. Wooden shims, which can be purchased at most home-improvement stores, are great for leveling a tank. For a metal stand, I have used folded paper many times. On a carpet it can be quite a trick to get it balanced. Do the best that you can now because it will pay off later.

Getting Tanked

Once the stand is in place and balanced, you can place the aquarium. There really is no trick to putting the tank on the stand. If the stand is level, the tank will be also. If you place the tank and find out it isn't quite level you should not prop up the spot where the aquarium is off. Take the tank off and rebalance the stand. You want as much of the aquarium bottom resting on the stand as possible. Raising up one corner or edge of the aquarium creates a point with a very small surface area that will be supporting a lot of weight. You want to distribute the weight across as much surface area as possible. All the weight on one point could lead to failure of the bottom of the tank–that means lots of water on the floor.

Be sure the aquarium is level when first placed on the stand as well as throughout the tank's life.

Grovel With the Gravel

Your next step is to place the gravel in the tank. Most gravel and substrate material should be rinsed before putting it in the tank. Most of the specialty substrates for planted tanks will seem quite dirty. Don't sweat getting all the debris out of it, I think that some of the smaller particles are good to leave in the substrate. My experience has been that even though it seems like the stuff will make a mess, it doesn't. The small particles settle out very quickly. Don't even bother rinsing laterite. It is a fine powder; plan on putting that in your tank dry.

Place the first layer of gravel to a depth of about 1 inch if you are using regular gravel. Add your layer of laterite and/or peat. If you use peat, make a thin layer. Now put another 2 inches of gravel on top, being very careful not to disturb the laterite or peat. Adding a small scoop at a time and carefully covering the laterite will help. If you are using a commercial substrate, just load it in. Dumping too much at once can be pretty hard on the glass bottom of the tank and could possible crack it. Adding small scoops will prevent any problems.

Water Water Everywhere

You can add your water either with a bucket a hose or a special aquarium water changer made specifically for the purpose. If you have chlorine or chloramines in your water now

Part 4

Be sure to add your gravel after placing heavy objects in the tank first.

is the time to add something to remove them. If you aren't sure it's best to just add something that will remove chloramines, it can't hurt and could save your fish. Some people like to use other water conditioners too.

There are two ways to go from here; you can either fill the tank partially with water, plant, and then finish filling, or just fill to the top then plant. Many people prefer the first method and find it easier.

For this method, first add water to the tank so that the water is just over the surface of the gravel. This saves you from getting your sleeves all wet as you reach down into the full tank to place the plants, and keeps the water from sloshing over the top when you put your hands in. Why not do it with the gravel completely dry? If the gravel is slightly submerged, it will act a little more "liquid." As you place the plants, the gravel will fall back into place nicely around the roots of the plant. Also if planting takes you a while it's good for the plants to have some moisture.

If your tank is second hand, or you tend to be nervous about even a slight possibility of water all over, it's a good idea to let your tank sit for several hours to make sure there are no leaks after you've put in a bit of water.

The second method is to just fill the tank to the top first; just be sure to at least leave an inch or so of unfilled space at the top. This is so the water that will be displaced when you put your hands in won't end up on your floor. There is no real problem doing your planting after most of the water is in place, it may be a little harder to see the bottom and carefully place the plants, but it does have the benefit of being able to see what the plants look like while they are floating in the water. Which method you use is pretty much up to you and really has no affect on the success of growing your plants.

When you add water to the tank, you will want to be very careful to avoid disturbing the substrate. If you have used laterite this is even more important. You want that laterite to stay in the bottom layer of the gravel. One good way to accomplish this is to place a saucer on the gravel and slowly run the water into the tank on top of the saucer. When the tank is about half full, you can remove the saucer and finish the job. If you're pretty handy or have two people you can just use your hand under the direct flow of water.

Hangin' the Hardware

You can also do this step before you add the water. It is really up to you. One reason to wait is that most aquarium heaters are made of glass. By waiting, you avoid bumping it and breaking it as you do your build. You can also save the heater for last for the same reason, unless of course you're using substrate heating, which should have gone in before the gravel.

The filter should be installed and started up the same day that you add water. You may have some cloudiness from the gravel. Getting your filter on the job early will get it cleaned up faster. Also, get the lights working if you have already planted your tank.

Start up on your CO_2 system will be a little more complicated. I recommend waiting a week or two before you start with CO_2. The tank will take some time to settle and you should begin testing the water parameters. A good understanding of your water is key to getting good results with CO_2 addition.

Bring On the Critters

Your tank is up and running and you can't wait to enter it in the photo contest! Well, maybe that will be in a few months. Let's talk about ways to get the plants going well and fish swimming healthy.

Aquatic Gardening

Placing your plants in the tank is your first chore as an aquatic gardener. You have probably worked out a scheme for arranging the plants in the tank. It is best to fully plant your new tank. Adding a few here and a few there will probably lead to frustration. By adding a good population of plants at the start, you will have enough there to work on out-competing the algae that will surely be present.

This gorgeous aquarium is a perfect home for many unique aquarium residents.

Specific instructions for planting and caring for your plants can be found in the following chapters. Here are some general recommendations.

• Remove any rubber bands, lead weights, or twist ties that are holding the bunch of plants together. Dispose of any lead weighs carefully and don't let your kids play with them.

• Trim away any dead material. You may need to trim away a few leaves on stem plants. You will need to bury several "nodes" where the roots will form. In a new tank, go ahead and place them in the substrate.

• Consider using a plastic mesh to arrange and hold down small plants. This technique can work well for small plants like the mosses and *Glossostigma elatinoides.*

As you are placing your plants, it is a good idea to place a fertilizer tablet in the gravel near the new plants. There are several good brands available on the market. I often break them into pieces and place a small amount near a newly planted specimen.

Bring On the Fish

You have probably done a lot of research to decide which plants you are going to keep. Please take the same amount of time researching your fish and other aquarium animals. Select species that will not eat your plants and will live peacefully together. You can keep some more aggressive fish in a community tank but the tank mates need to be too big to be eaten and fast enough to get away from the aggressor. For example, I keep some cichlids in my planted tank with several tetras and barbs. Neons or other small tetras would be eaten by the cichlids in this tank, so I don't buy any.

The Siamese flying fox is one fish that will help keep your aquarium algae free.

Unfortunately, tropical fish are often kept in suboptimal conditions before they arrive at your home. Many importers and stores use a system that has a central filter system. That means that many of the tanks are connected and any fish that is sick can spread it to all

Part 4

the other fish in the system. Carefully inspect the fish in the store before you bring them home. Don't try to rescue a sad, sick fish, leave it at the store. If you bring it home, it will almost assuredly die and take some of your other fish with it.

If you can, the very best thing to do is keep a fish-only quarantine aquarium. Any new fish can spend their first few weeks with you under close observation for disease before being introduced into your show tank. All of the things you know about the nitrogen cycle will apply to your quarantine tank. It is best to have an established tank set up as your quarantine.

Most people probably don't quarantine the fish, though they should. Fish from pet stores are often exposed to a plethora of diseases and are under stress, they can bring a horrible plague to your tank that can wipe out the whole thing. I don't mean to sound extreme but it does happen and if you don't quarantine fish for a community tank it very likely will happen. New fish should either go in a tank of their own or be quarantined for a couple weeks before adding to a community tank. Keep a very good eye on the fish while being quarantined to make sure that they are doing fine.

You can put your very first fish in your new tank without quarantining but subsequent fish should be quarantined first. Take your new bag of fish and float the bag in the top of your tank. Let them float for a half hour to equalize the temperature between the bag and the tank. Just before you cut open the bag and release the fish, give your existing fish a small feeding. This will keep their attention away from the new

To keep your fish healthy, quarantine all new comers. *Epiplatys dageti* are pictured

African clawed frogs also make nice additions to planted tanks.

Part 4

additions. After you open the bag, add a little of your tank water to the water in the bag. Wait a little while, now release the new fish. Most fish are pretty sturdy and can handle the change in water conditions they will be experiencing when they move into your tank. Watch the newcomers for awhile to make sure they settle down and are not harassed by their tank mates.

Passing the Test

Now that you have added fish, start testing the ammonia and nitrite levels every few days. Since the tank will have lots of plants, you may never see the levels go up that much. The plants can use the nitrogenous wastes as fertilizer right away.

Housekeeping for Your Underwater Garden

Finally, after a lot of hard work, you have a new aquatic garden. The aquascape is beautiful; the tank is full of healthy growing plants. The fish look nice playing tag around the driftwood and some may even have babies! Great job! You probably feel pretty good about your accomplishments.

It would be nice about now to sit down beside your aquarium with a tall glass of iced tea and admire your handiwork. Go right ahead. Just don't get too comfortable.

You will need to do a few regular chores to keep everything beautiful and clean. Why bother? For several reasons. The first is that your fish are

In time, your own aquatic garden may look like this one.

counting on you. They are swimming in a closed system. Even with the nitrogen cycle and the plants working in your favor, there are some dissolved chemicals that will not be converted. Nitrate, tannins, and even some fish hormones may be in the water. After awhile you may see some little piles of mulm building up in the corners. Your filter will work well, but it will also need a rinse to remove the solids that accumulate.

Regular trimming, pruning, and replanting are needed to keep your underwater garden beautiful. Once your plants get going they can very rapidly get out of hand without regular maintenance. Stemmed plants often quickly grow to the top of the tank and over it. They need to be pruned and replanted regularly. Sword plants will sometimes need older dying leaves trimmed as new ones fill the center. Slow growing crypts can sneak up and take over large sections of the aquarium. *Vallisneria*, *Sagittaria*, and *Najas* will send runners all over the tank, not always where you want them. I'll discuss the different techniques for trimming the different types of plants in plant sections.

Aquarium chores can be very pleasant and relaxing. It's a quit and peaceful pastime, and can be a line to nature even in the heart of the city. I like to garden, and caring for my aquatic garden is relaxing and fun for me. I know many people who did not grow up gardening who absolutely hate garden chores at first. Even these nay-sayers find that they actually relax and feel a sense of accomplishment with their new hobby.

Do Your Chores

You may find it easiest to make a list of chores. You can go through this list every time you are ready to do your aquarium chores. I will also tell you how often to perform each chore. In time your aquarium chores will become like second nature.

Daily Chores

• Feed the fish a good quality diet. Remember, don't over feed.

• Inspect your fish for any signs of illness. Sores, refusing to eat, and little movement are not good signs.

• Check your plants. Have any been dug up? Are they growing well? Look green (or red) and healthy?

- Remove any dead plant parts and replant anything that is floating.

- Check your equipment. Is everything running properly?

- Check your filter. Is it running slowly? Are the filter pads clogged?

- Check your CO_2 system. Do you see bubbles coming from your compressed gas or fermentation system?

Weekly Chores

Once a week you will need to devote a little more time to your aquarium. It won't take too long–about an hour.

- This is a great time to check your water chemistry. Check pH, ammonia, and nitrite.

- Hook up your siphon and begin your water change.

- Use the siphon to remove any debris that has accumulated on the surface of the substrate. You can usually do this easily without disturbing the plants too much.

- Clean your power filter. Rinse the pads and sponges in clean water to remove any accumulated solids.

- Refill the tank and check your pH, KH and dGH. Make any chemical additions that are needed to put your water back in your operation point. Use water dechlorinator as needed.

- Add nutrients for the plants as needed. I usually dose with a good trace mineral supplement every water change.

- Restart the filter.

Must Do Chore – Change the Water

Regular partial water changes are a crucial part of keeping your tank healthy. It is simple, and fresh water replacement will prevent most of the most common aquarium problems.

Listen to me: water changes are good, water changes are easy. Your fish and plants love water changes. I think you are starting to get the idea that I am a big fan of water changes.

Why Keep the Water Clean?

Clean water will save you so much trouble later on. Really, trust me. You must keep your water clean and keep up with regular partial water changes. It always amazes me how many people disregard this advice. This is the best advice I can give. Clean water will prevent sick fish, prevent algae overgrowth, and replenish trace minerals that the plants have used.

The Benefits of New Water

Regular partial water changes will have the following benefits for your aquarium:

• Dissolved wastes will be removed and diluted.

• Nitrates will be removed.

• Depleted minerals will be replaced.

In addition, your fish will have brighter colors and will grow better. I have heard it said that some fish give off hormones that inhibit the growth of other fish. I don't know if it is true, but it may make some sense. If a large male fish can inhibit the size of his rivals, his chances of mating could be increased.

How to Change Your Water

Changing the water in your tank means taking out the old and putting in new. Just topping up water that has evaporated will not help much. The amount of water you change depends on the frequency of the changes. A minimum of 20 percent of the tank volume per week up to 50 percent per week should be your goal. I favor doing large water changes and do at least 50 percent every week.

Take the Old Water Out

The easiest way to change the water is to use a siphon. There are several brands of aquarium siphons that attach to a sink and do double duty. Look for a siphon that has a rigid tube on the end for cleaning the bottom of the tank. Make sure that the hose is long enough to reach your sink or drain. As you use the siphon to remove water, gently use the rigid tube at the base of your plants and above the gravel to remove mulm and other debris. Don't disturb the gravel bed with the siphon in your planted tank. The plant roots are sensitive and the debris that is deeper in the gravel won't harm the plants.

Put New Water In

Refill your tank with tap water that has been adjusted to the correct temperature. Adding very cold water will shock and even kill sensitive fish. You can add dechlorinator directly to the tank before you add the new tap water. It will react with the new water to remove chlorine immediately.

Use your test kit to measure the KH and pH of the tank water. Make the needed additions of buffers to return your tank to the correct KH and pH. When the pH and KH are correct, add any fertilizers as needed.

If you cannot use your tap water directly, you can prepare your new water in a clean plastic container that you use only for this chore. A new plastic garbage can will work nicely. There are several advantages for preparing your water in a separate container. You can use dechlorinator (if needed), adjust the hardness and pH and add any fertilizer chemicals to the replacement water. Using a separate container allows you to be more precise with the new water and do less water testing.

Dissolved Gasses in New Water

The new water that you add to the aquarium, whether it is city water or well water, may not have very much dissolved oxygen in it. If you are doing a large water change and there is not enough oxygen in the water, the fish may become stressed. You can spray the new water at the top of the tank to mix in some oxygen. It can be tricky to do this and not spray down the wall but you will get the hang of it.

If you detect a problem with your water quality, you should increase the frequency and quantity of water that you change. Ten percent every day or 20 percent three times a week will get the water back in shape within two weeks.

Nutrient Addition for Your Plants

Nutrient dosing is a widely debated topic with aquatic gardeners. The basic rationale behind it is this–in a closed system, the growth of the plants will be limited by something;

Part 4

light, CO_2, macronutrients, or micronutrients. When your aquarium has high light and plenty of CO_2 you may find that it does become depleted of the macronutrients, nitrogen, phosphorus, or potassium. In this case, you may consider using a product to put a small amount of these elements back in the tank. For most, it is a matter of adding the nutrients slowly and observing the benefit. There is no problem with keeping your tank this way; however, it will be time intensive to dose the tank daily. If you are seeking a really intensive culture of aquatic plants, get plugged into some of the Internet resources to learn the ins and outs of daily dosing.

You can certainly keep your plants growing and healthy without large doses of fertilizer. I personally prefer a more low-key approach. I place fertilizer tablets in the substrate that contains the macronutrients and dose weekly with a good trace mineral supplement. With any fertilizer tablet, make sure that it is made for aquatic plants and is "timed release." I have used pond tabs and planted aquarium tablets with good results.

Keeping Up With CO_2

We discussed the use of CO_2 and it has been shown that even lower light tanks can benefit from CO_2 use. You will need to keep an eye on the usage of CO_2 in your tank. You will need to periodically recharge your fermenter or gas bottle. Remember that the pH of your tank will go higher when you run out of CO_2. In most cases, this should cause your fish no distress but it is best to be aware of the chemistry and monitor your fish's behavior.

Enjoy and Grow

I don't want your chores to become something that is a drudge for you. Remember that you will be spending most of your time observing your plants and animals and enjoying your beautiful landscape. Doing a few chores once a week will probably be easier in the long run than a big job less often. The plants and fish will benefit too. Hey, and you can always sell all those plant babies to your other aquatic gardening friends. I hope that you really enjoy your new hobby and that you are proud of your artistic creation.

Part 4

Part Five

Fish and Other Animals

"Oh great guru! I have travled far! What is the meaning of Life?"

Fish for the Planted Tank

There are several factors to consider when choosing fishes for your planted aquarium. Many of the fish often offered for the aquarium are also suitable for the planted tank, but some fishes are definitely not compatible.

Some species are herbivores that need to have a large part, or all, of their diet made up of plant-based matter. This isn't a big problem and can actually be beneficial if the greenery they prefer happens to be algae or decaying plant mater. But if these fishes happen to be large, watch out. Some species, like silver dollars, can plow through your lovely underwater paradise like a cow at the salad bar.

Many fishes are suitable for inclusion in your aquatic garden.

Characodon sp, Durango

Other fishes like to create their own environment by moving the gravel and rocks around. These fishes are often not suitable for the standard planted aquarium, though there are tricks to include plants in tanks with some of these species, as long as they aren't too big and can't cause too much destruction. Generally, larger fishes are not suitable for a planted aquarium anyway.

Which Fish to Choose?

There are large numbers of suitable fishes for the planted aquarium. If this is your first tank, you may want to browse through your local fish stores and see what fish you are most interested in then look them up in books to see if they will fit in with your aquarium design plans. Choosing your fish carefully will go a long way to insure your success with them. If you have previous experience, you may already know what fish you would like to have in your tank.

For most home aquariums, it's usually best to have a small number of different types of fish in one tank; one to three is usually enough. Choosing them carefully can help avoid conflicts and deaths in the future. Choose species that will either get along with one another or won't be interested in each other. Guppies and platies with *Corydoras* would make a nice, easy mix, as would a school of zebras or white clouds with a group of small tetras and a small algae eater.

Many single fish are more likely to become mean or be picked on by other species than they would if they were housed in groups of their own kind. Still, there will always be exceptions, and some fish have different temperaments than others. Watch your fish regularly so that you can spot problems before they become fatal.

Fish Families

Fish, like other animals, are generally categorized into groups based on similarities between individual types. There are specific and scientific ways to classify fish and other animals. These basic classifications are Kingdom, Phylum, Class, Order, Family, Genus, and Species. Scientists can further classify organisms into subphyla, subclasses, suborders, subfamilies, subgenera, and of course, subspecies. These classifications aren't carved in stone, and new information from detailed studying of the animals in question can change the classification.

If it seems a bit confusing, that's because it is. Even scientists don't always agree on how some plants and animals should be organized. You may be wondering how this can help you. Generally, animals in the same groupings have similarities, so knowledge about one can help you understand the relationships and attributes of different animals.

Even with the occasional name changes, the scientific names are often the best way to refer to fish to avoid confusion, as common names can be regional, and several fish may have the same common name.

A good example of an animal name change that received international attention was that of the dinosaur *Brontosaurus,* which was changed to *Apatosaurus*. The name wasn't really changed; rather, it was a correction to an error in the original naming of the animal, but the *Brontosaurus* had already become a popular dinosaur by that name. These sorts of name changes happen regularly, but not often with such well-known animals.

Carps and Minnows

Some of the most well-known representatives of these groups are the tiger barb (*Puntius tetrazona*) and the zebra danio (*Danio rerio*), both named for their similarity to the coloration of the well-known mammals. Harlequin rasboras (*Rasbora heteromorpha*), cherry barbs (*Puntius titeya*), and the White Cloud Mountain minnow (*Tanichthys albonubes*) are other very common and similar fishes that are all suitable for the planted aquarium. Quite a few others are regularly available, too.

Goldfish are closely related to carp, and though they are a popular aquarium fish, they are not generally suitable for the planted aquarium. Goldfish enjoy eating many plants and will usually destroy and eat those placed in the same tank with them.

Most of the small, suitable fishes in this group are

Small barbs are good fish to have in your planted tank.

generally happiest in groups. Six or more is often a good number, because fewer fish can lead to nipped fins of other tank inhabitants—some of these fish can get quite mean if left alone or in small groups. These fish will often lay eggs in the aquarium, but unless some care is taken or the tank is very heavily planted with a small population of fish, the eggs will not often survive.

Characins

Another group of fishes that likes to swim in schools are the characins. They include the often beautifully-colored tetras and can be identified by the small extra fin just before the tail, which is called an adipose fin. These fish make lovely additions to the planted aquarium with their splashy and metallic colors. Cardinal tetras (*Paracheirodon axelrodi*) are among the most colorful of the small schooling fishes. Pencil fishes and hatchet fishes are also included among the characins, along with many others.

Most of these fishes prefer soft, acid water. Their natural waters are often dark and referred to as "black water." The bright metallic colors of these little fishes show through the water, despite its dark characteristics. Like barbs and danios, characins will often lay eggs in the aquarium, but the fry will usually not survive unless there are ample hiding places with few predators or set breeding procedures are followed.

Catfishes

Catfishes can be another wonderful addition to the planted aquarium. Many of them mix well with other fish, since they tend to like the bottom of the tank, where other fish don't usually frequent.

Cardinal tetras are very popular residents of aquatic gardens.

Small armored catfishes make good janitors for aquatic gardens.

Corydoras species are among the favorites of aquarium fishes. Other small catfishes, including the interesting upside-down catfish (*Synodontis* sp.) and some small plecostomus-type species, will also live comfortably in a planted aquarium. When choosing these, make sure they stay small and will not outgrow the confines of your aquarium. Larger plecostomus species are likely to enjoy your plantings as a wonderful snack tray.

Many catfishes can be bred in the aquarium, though care must usually be taken for fry to survive. Since these fish generally stay near the bottom of the tank, always make sure that they're getting enough food. Some of these fishes like to hide, so you may not see them often, but others spend a great deal of time at the front of the tank. Be sure to research the fish you're interested in to achieve the best results in mixing fishes.

Cichlids

Though many of the large cichlids are not appropriate for the planted aquarium, some cichlids do very well with plants. Small cichlids from South America and Africa can coexist with them quite peacefully. The *Apistogramma, Mikrogeophagus,* and *Pelvicachromis* genera contain many species of small cichlids and are usually quite suitable to house in planted aquariums. Some larger cichlids like discus (*Symphysodon* spp.) and angelfishes (*Pterophyllum* spp.) are also appropriate for the planted tank.

Some of the marginal fishes can be kept in planted tanks with special arrangements. Planting in pots and using plants with stronger leaves can sometimes discourage fish

Oto Cats

Otocinclus species are very small catfishes that have gained in popularity in recent years. They will eat some types of algae. They are very non aggressive fish and will live comfortably with many other species, though they can be somewhat sensitive in moving. You should be particularly careful to quarantine them after purchase, before they go into a tank with other fish. Once established, they generally do well as long as they have enough food. Be careful to watch that they are not only eating but look well fed. If there isn't enough algae growing in the tank to support them, they should be supplemented with a sinking algae-based fish food.

Blue rams are excellent additions to your planted aquarium.

American Flag Fish

American flag fish (*Jordanella floridae*) are a killifish species that is native to Florida. These fish are often recommended as algae-eating fish; they will even eat bothersome hair algae.

American flag fish are attractive with their flashy blue and red markings, and the males can be particularly appealing. These fish breed easily in the aquarium and don't molest their fry. The male flag fish can become aggressive toward other fish and some aquarists recommend keeping only females in a community tank.

from destroying plants. With most of the large cichlids, though, there really isn't a practical way of keeping both fishes and plants in the same tank.

Cichlids can be very interesting fishes. They often form pairs and share in the responsibility of raising eggs and fry. These fishes often exhibit more of a personality than some of the smaller schooling fishes, and can be territorial and aggressive. Do your research when choosing cichlids.

Killifish

Killifishes are great little fishes that are underutilized in the commercial aquarium world. Some of these fishes can be extremely colorful and attractive.

Many of the most colorful killies are annuals; they live in places where the water dries up. The fishes die when the water is gone, but the eggs remain and hatch again when the waters return.

There are also many killifish that lay eggs that hatch in water like other fishes. Many can live with the fry and young in a multi generational aquarium.

Labyrinths

The labyrinths, or "anabantids," offered for the aquarium are generally medium to small fishes, though there are larger fishes in the group. Labyrinth fishes are generally slender, tall, very attractive fish; males can be particularly colorful. This group includes the ever-popular betta, also known as the Siamese fighting fish, as well as gouramis and paradise fishes.

Labyrinth fishes have several interesting features.

Bettas do well in aquariums that are heavily planted.

They have developed a special organ that allows them to live in poorly oxygenated waters called the labyrinth organ, and it allows them to obtain oxygen from the air. Not surprisingly, most of these fishes spend the majority of their time near the surface. Most also build unique bubble nests at the top of the tank; these nests are created by the males and often include floating plants or pieces of plants. Labyrinths often breed readily in the home aquarium, and the males usually raise the fry alone.

Labyrinths make excellent fishes for the planted aquarium. With the proper care, they can also do well in a community tank. They are often very aggressive with other labyrinths, particularly males, and can sometimes be aggressive to other fish. Surprisingly, though, they are more often the victims of aggression from their tankmates. They are often surprisingly easy for other fishes to bully, especially considering their fierceness toward each other.

Livebearers

Livebearers include the ever-popular guppies, mollies, swordtails, and platies. Usually the fishes found in pet stores are highly-colored. These have been carefully bred for many generations to produce the varieties that are now available.

The fancy varieties offered at the pet stores had to come from somewhere, and their wild ancestors and related species are also great for the planted tank. While some livebearers can be plain, some are also very attractive. *Brachyrhaphis holdridgei* is a beautiful orange and purple fish, and perhaps the most strikingly attractive wild livebearer.

Platys come in many different color varieties.

Fancy guppies are always a popular choice.

Algae Eaters

Another fish that's grouped with the loaches is the Siamese algae eater. These fish are very popular with planted tank aquarists for their algae-eating abilities and have been known to munch on annoying hair algae. Similar fish are often available, so sometimes identifying them can be confusing. Flying foxes, another similar-looking fish, are sometimes confused with the Siamese algae eater, but they often won't eat your algae so don't make the mistake of purchasing one for that purpose.

Some livebearers are considered helpful algae eaters, the most common of these being the molly. Perhaps the most often recommended algae-eating livebearer is the *Ameca splendens*. These fish are called goodieds, and many of them will usually eat some algae. These fish are, like the killies, somewhat harder to find, but are sometimes available through pet stores, fish clubs, or other hobbyists.

As the name implies, livebearer fry are born alive. They are often very easy to breed. Multi-generational families are often possible in the home aquarium. Many fry often survive in a well-planted tank, though more fry will be lost in a community aquarium. Livebearers are usually good community fishes and do great in the home aquarium.

Loaches

Loaches are an interesting group of fishes. Generally, these species live toward the bottom of the aquarium. Many of them are very suitable for the planted aquarium and make wonderful members of community tanks.

Kuhli loaches are small, long loaches with dark stripes on a light body, though some are entirely dark and have variable striping. These cute little fish love to congregate in large groups under aquarium ornaments like wood and rocks. You may not see them a great deal.

Several *Botia* species are often available as well. One of these is the clown loach (*Chromobotia macracantha*), which is another popular striped fish. Most *Botia* are very effective at eating snails. This can be bad or good depending on how you feel about snails in your tanks. Some species of *Botia* will make clicking sounds to each other. This, among other behavior, is very interesting to observe with this group.

The Praecox Rainbowfish makes a colorful statement as it swims about the garden.

Rainbowfishes

Rainbows and blue eyes are often very attractive, colorful, and active fishes that are very popular as planted tank inhabitants. They range in size from small to medium sized fish. These fish look lovely in their flashy schools, swimming among the plants. Colors include reds and blues, though males can look much different than females. *Glossolepis incisus,* for example, is a larger rainbow species in which the males are a brilliant red. Sometimes available is a particularly lovely, but difficult to care for, fish–the feather-fin rainbow, *Iriatherina werneri.*

Most rainbows are much easier to care for, though, and will also breed readily in the home aquarium. Occasionally fry will survive in the community tank. Care should be taken because some of these fish may crossbreed in the tank; a practice generally frowned on by hobbyists.

Some extreme hobbyists have many, many aquariums filled with all sorts of goodies.

Though these fish can be kept in a community tank, remember with all fish that individuals may differ and care must be taken in choosing which fish to include in one particular tank. In general, fish of similar sizes and compatible temperaments should be kept together. Remember to consider the full-grown size–not just the current size–of a fish.

Now Try to Pick Just a Few

With so many wonderful fishes available to the planted aquarist, the biggest problem is to choose just a few. This is why many successful hobbyists have several tanks. Remember, the most important thing in choosing compatible species is to research the individual species you would like to include.

Shrimps and Snails and Bug Larva Tails

Invertebrates are animals that don't have a back bone. Insects are the ones you probably notice most often. Shrimp, crabs, snails, slugs, and worms are also all invertebrates.

Invertebrates make up the majority of animals on the earth, approximately 95 percent, so it's no surprise that you can find them in your aquarium too. Some of the invertebrates you can find in your aquarium live only part of their lives in the water, while others are aquatic their entire lives.

Choosing Invertebrates

Some invertebrates make interesting tank inhabitants, with fish or alone. Others can

An aquatic garden such as this could be home to a wide diversity of freshwater invertebrates.

actually be helpful in the care of your fish tank, particularly in the area of algae removal. Some are used for fish food and others are unwelcome visitors that hitch a ride in with your plants.

Shrimp

Shrimp, crayfish, and crabs are all decapods. These are 10-legged crustaceans. Most of these animals live in the ocean with their relative the lobster, but some live in freshwater and are not only suitable but desirable in the planted aquarium.

Several species of shrimp have been sporadically available to hobbyists in the past. One species in particular, *Caridina japonica*, is more commonly available to the aquarium hobbyist. In the past, they were hard to come by but they have now gained popularity in recent years due to their prominence in various aquarium literature and their stunning photographs in the *Nature Aquarium World* books written by Mr. Takashi Amano. These shrimp, sometimes dubbed the "Amano shrimp," are used to help control some types of algae.

Years ago, the only shrimp readily available in the United States was generally the ghost shrimp, a *Palaemon* species usually sold as a feeder shrimp for large fish. The ghost shrimp also proved to be effective at eating some kinds of algae. Several different shrimp have started to become available to aquarists now, including the Amano shrimp. It's an exciting new area for hobbyists to explore.

Shrimp suitable for the freshwater planted aquarium are a group of similar decapods with long, hard-shelled bodies. They have a pair of front legs called chelipeds, equipped with tooled claws; these are what the shrimp use to get the algae in your tank. The front legs are followed by 4 pairs of walking legs called pereiopods. Under the shrimp's abdomen they have swimmerets that can aid in swimming and egg care in the females. Shrimp eyes are compound and almost always stalked. The shrimp have two pairs of antenna and several other appendages

Various species of shrimp have gained considerable popularity in recent years.

coming from the head area that give them a very interesting appearance.

There may be some question as to the identity of some of these shrimp as they are rather new to the hobby. Hopefully their identification will be clearer in the near future. There are also many more shrimp that may be suitable for the home aquarium and availability will probably improve.

It's good to remember that in the wild there's a lot of eat or be eaten and care should be taken when choosing tank mates. If you're interested in keeping small shrimp, be sure any fish you are planning on putting with them are small and won't consider your shrimp a tasty hors d'oeuvre. The same care should be taken if choosing to keep larger clawed shrimp that may consider your fish a nice little sardine snack.

Just like fish your shrimp will need food to survive. Most shrimp are purchased to help control aquarium algae. However not all shrimp will eat all kinds of algae. Watch your shrimp and be sure they are eating something. Feeding shrimp can be a touchy thing. If you have a lot of algae in your tank that the shrimp will eat, then you don't want to feed them a lot of other foods that will keep them from eating the algae. However if you have a lot of shrimp and there is no algae left they will have to be fed. Most will eat some form of fish food. If they are algae eating shrimp feed them foods high in algae content that can get to their level. Sinking foods are more likely to reach the shrimp before the fish eat it all.

Some shrimp prefer a more varied diet and would prefer food with a little more meat in it. Sinking fish foods can be helpful. There are also new foods out that are specifically for shrimp and crabs. Some shrimp are predatory and will catch fish with their claws.

The shrimp grow with all that eating, but their shells don't. So they must shed their old shells for new ones periodically. The shrimp are usually vulnerable at this time. It takes time for the new shells to harden. The amount of time it takes depends on the type of shrimp. If you see what looks like a dead shrimp in your tank, it may just be a shell. They come off in one large piece and look like your shrimp.

Caridina
The popular Amano shrimp, *C. japonica*, is a member of this genus. The Amano shrimp are native to Japan, and other Asian countries as many of the shrimp coming in to the

Amano shrimp, *Caridina japonica*, is a popular algae eating shrimp.

Many of the smaller shrimp are easily confused with each other.

aquarium hobby are. Amano shrimp often stay in a group and walk over the tank looking for food, though sometimes they separate and are seen individually. Females are larger than males and it's not unusual to see them holding eggs under their abdomen in their swimmerets. Unfortunately they are rather difficult to raise the young. In nature they are swept out to sea to mature before going back to the freshwater. Some accounts of successful raising of fry have been reported if they are raised in strongly brackish water.

There are other shrimp in this genus that are becoming available. Some of them are very attractive, like the bumblebee shrimp, *C. serrata*. Though there may be several shrimp being sold under the name of bumblebee and some may be *Neocaridina* species. These are attractive small algae eating shrimp with stripes. Special care should be taken in choosing tank mates for very small shrimp. Some of these shrimp are reportedly easy to breed in the aquarium. Another very attractive shrimp, the crystal red or ninja, may have been selectively bred from members of this genus.

Neocaridina

The *Neocaridina* shrimp available for the aquarist is often similar to the *Caridina* and there may be some confusion in the hobby as to which exact shrimp are in which genus. The two genuses are in the same family, Atyidae.

Neocaridina reportedly produce larger eggs than *Caridina,* which is a way to distinguish them. Some members of both genuses are able to breed in the aquarium. The female shrimp carries the eggs and developing fry. The shrimp release the developing fry when they've become miniature versions of their parents, making them relatively easy to raise. Fry usually can eat smaller pieces of the same things their parents eat.

Some of the attractive shrimp that may be available in this genus are the tiger, blue, and red cherry shrimp. I prefer the red cherry shrimp, *Neocaridina denticulata*. These are very colorful small shrimp that spend all day eating algae and seem to be hardier than other varieties.

Palaemon

A shrimp that has been readily available to most North American aquarists for some time is a native shrimp, the ghost shrimp. These animals are usually sold as feeder shrimp for large fish, but they have the added benefit of eating algae. These shrimp are rather plain and clear which gave them the name ghost shrimp. They are also sometimes called glass or grass shrimp. There may be a few different species going under these names. These shrimp can be effective in eating hair algae and breed quite easily in the aquarium. Shrimp fry will be eaten by the fish and probably the adult shrimp. In an aquarium with peaceful fish and a great deal of plant life for the shrimp fry to hide in, then some should survive.

Another Palaemon that's starting to become available is the South American *P. scarletti*. This shrimp is also called the red fronted, or red nosed shrimp, and can have red stripes on its rather long rostrum, and body. The Malaysian Rainbow shrimp *P. hendersoni* and other *Palaemon* are also sometimes available to aquarists.

The red-nosed shrimp is being imported regularly now.

Macrobrachium

Some members of this genus are used for shrimp farming and end up on the dinner table, but occasionally they are available for the aquarium. These shrimp have long arms with claws. Be sure to consider the adult size of the shrimp and its claws before deciding if they should be kept with your fish. Some would enjoy a fish kabob lunch, and are capable of for catching small fish. They can also be aggressive to each other and some may be territorial. *Macrobrachium* shrimp that may be available are the red spotted shrimp, chameleon shrimp (*M. pilimanus*), red claw shrimp (*M. assamensis*), and sunset shrimp (*M. idella*).

Atyopsis

Sold under names such as Wood, Bamboo, Thai, or Singapore Shrimp, these are very attractive filter feeders that can grow up to 3 inches long. These lovely shrimp from Singapore are not a threat to fish despite their size. Instead of the standard claw they have fans on their front legs that filter their food out of the water. This shrimp is a nice brown color with tan stripes. Since they can only eat tiny foods strained out of the aquarium water they can be difficult to feed. They seem to do very well in green water.

Crayfish

Crayfish are regularly offered for sale to the aquarist. Sometimes they are also called freshwater lobsters. You might think that because of their similarity to shrimp they might be a good candidate for your planted aquarium; however, they really aren't. Most crayfish will consider your lovely plants a tasty salad. Those big pinchers work great for lopping off plants. They are also good at pulling them out, too. There are large numbers of different types of crayfish. They also come in a variety of colors from green to brown and red and even blue. They are very interesting animals and fun to keep but not generally in the planted tank.

Crayfish can be very destructive to your planted aquarium!

Crabs

There are generally two types of crabs that are somewhat regularly offered for sale for the freshwater aquarium. They are red claw crabs and fiddler crabs.

Red claw crabs (*Sesarma bidens*) are very attractive, usually red, orange, and purple in color. These little crabs are relatively easy to keep in the aquarium if you can keep them contained. They do like to escape and are very good at doing so. They may be able to live under water at all times, though they do seem to enjoy air time also. Red claw crabs seem to be more content in a tank where they have a place they can get out of the water, even if it is a small space.

Some fiddler crabs prefer brackish over fresh water. Males have the larger "fiddle" claw. They have been reported to occasionally breed in the aquarium, but it's pretty much impossible to raise the larva. They can also be territorial and a larger tank may be needed to provide enough space for several crabs. Fiddler crabs need places where they can come up out of the water. They can also eat some plants and might not be appropriate in most planted tanks.

Snails and Other Mollusks

Snails and limpets have a single coiled, one piece shell, while clams and other bivalves have two piece hinged shells. New shell growth on snails and limpets occurs at the outermost part of the coil. Some of them have round shells, some flat, and some are like a cone with a point.

Snails are interesting animals that have a large muscular foot with slime glands to help them crawl. On their head, above their eyes, they have a pair of tentacles that can extend and retreat. They have round mouths with a row of teeth that are replaced as they wear down while feeding on dead plants and animals.

There are two main types of snails; gilled snails (Prosobranchs) and Pulmonate snails, which have lungs. In addition to having lungs the Pulmonate snails have a visibly different physical characteristic. They have a door-like plate attached to their foot called an operculum.

Not all snails are unwanted. This decorative golden snail is desirable for its size and color.

If you read older aquarium books and articles you may find several types of snails mentioned that aren't available today. They seemed to wane in popularity in the 70s, 80s and 90s but are gaining favor once again. A few new interesting snails are starting to become available at some specialty aquarium shops.

Gilled Snails

The snails most often found in the aquarium are the gilled snails. These snails usually show up in most aquariums whether they are wanted or not. Ramshorns, pond snails, and Malayan livebearing snails are the most common names of those types most often encountered.

Gilled snails can be hermaphroditic in several different ways depending on the species. Some change their sex, some cross fertilize each others eggs and some can fertilize their own eggs. Usually the eggs are seen as a little jelly like blob with tiny white dots. The Malayan livebearing snail is an exception. Anyway around it, they can achieve large populations rather quickly.

Ramshorns and Pond Snails

Generally of the two of these, it's the ramshorn that will come into the aquarium. Pond snails are less likely encountered in tanks in the house though they are much more common in outside ponds.

Some aquarists don't care for snails in their tanks and will go to almost any means available to rid their aquariums of them. There are sometimes rumors of these snails attacking healthy plants but usually the plants are in poor health before the snails started munching on them. However with the large number of small species, occasionally some of those that prefer plants may find their way into the aquarium. Generally the snails that are in most aquariums will prefer algae, detritus, and fish food to your prize aquarium plants.

Red ramshorns are those most often desired by planted aquarium enthusiasts. Since ramshorns is basically the style of shell and can include many different species these snails can be many different shapes, colors, and sizes, though they are generally small and some shade of brown, sometimes with spots. Pond snails have a longer spiraled shell and are also brown.

Malayan Livebearing Snail

These snails are rather unusual in that they don't lay eggs. They will breed very easily in the fish tank and will become well populated. They have very long cone shaped bodies, but they do stay rather small. They don't bother healthy plants and are safe for the planted tank.

Malayan livebearing snails are good at cleaning the gravel and often spend a great deal of their time digging through it. They aren't limited to the bottom of the tank though and will crawl through other areas. They can also learn when dinner time is and will often go to the top of the tank as soon as the fish are fed.

Pulmonate Snails

The large attractive aquarium snails, like apple snails and Colombian ramshorns are pulmonate snails. There are a lot of others in the wild but apple snails and Colombian ramshorns are those most often encountered in the aquarium trade.

Getting Rid of Snails

Some people just don't like snails and will try to remove them, dipping plants and using chemicals to eradicate snails and eggs. Snails are very hard to keep out of the tank and generally do more good than harm. I think the methods to get rid of the snails are worse than the actual snails, so I keep mine. Snails do a great job of keeping nuisance algae off tank surfaces, and I can't imagine my tanks without them.

Still, if you're dead set against snails, there is a biological way to help control them. This is with the use of a Botia. These are a group of loaches some of which are common to the aquarium trade. Some more easily found Botia are the clown, skunk, and yo-yo loaches.

Pulmonate snails will often breed in the aquarium. They usually lay eggs in jelly like bundles on sticks or branches above the water, though sometimes in the water.

These snails have an interesting feature called an operculum. This is a trapdoor like separate piece of shell. The snails can close this when they're inside their shells.

Apple or Mystery Snails

Some of these snails can be very helpful in the aquarium. The apple and mystery snails are lovely and attractive and do very well if they have adequate food. Most of the snails sold in shops won't bother healthy plants and will eat some types of algae.

These snails are sold in several color varieties. They have interesting, retractable breathing tubes that they use to get oxygen from above the water surface. If they have no way to get oxygen, say in a very full covered tank, they will eventually die.

Apple snails can often be bred in the aquarium. Most of these snails prefer to lay their eggs above the water so small branches or similar items must be placed in the aquarium that the snail can crawl out on to. Sometimes they may lay eggs on the sides or cover of an aquarium, above the water surface.

Most of the snails sold as apple snails or mystery snails in the pet shops are in fact wonderful additions to the aquarium. Occasionally other snails may be mistakenly brought in as there are a lot of them and they are similar in appearance. If you happen to get a snail that attacks healthy plants remove, it from the aquarium.

Colombian Ramshorn

These are commonly found in the aquarium trade. In shape they look like very large versions of the common brown ramshorn snails. In color they are usually striped various shades of tan and brown. Colombian ramshorns will lay eggs in the aquarium often on floating plants. They have a reputation for eating plants in the aquarium, though they can be kept with some tough leaved plants. In general they may not be a best first choice for the planted aquarium.

Other Mollusks

Occasionally fresh water clams are offered for sale for the aquarium. These animals don't really do much but sit in the gravel or substrate. They are filter feeders, meaning they eat tiny things floating in the water that they filter through their bodies. They can help clean out the water but it needs to be reasonably full of food for them to survive for any length of time. The do tend to do well in a tank of green water.

Hydras and Moss Animals

Hydras and moss animals are small invertebrates that occasionally show up in the aquarium. If you see them they will be tiny multitentacled animals usually found on the plants or the sides of the aquarium. Both hydra and moss animals are fairly harmless in the community aquarium, but may eat the small fry of egg laying fish in a breeding tank.

Hydras are from the family of invertebrates known as Coelenterata. The most well-known animals from this family are the anemones, coral, and jellyfish that make their homes in the oceans. There are also a small number of these invertebrates that live in fresh water. They are generally very small, individually living animals with tiny tentacles. They are pale colors, usually white, but can be tinted tan or green, and can sometimes be somewhat translucent.

Hydras use their tentacles to catch prey of other tiny invertebrates. They have also been reported to sometimes eat very small new fish fry. These animals can reproduce in the aquarium either sexually, forming a single egg or more commonly asexually by forming buds. Some gouramis will eat hydra.

Most of the moss animals are also found in the ocean but there are some that live in fresh water. They can be distinguished from hydras in the aquarium by their colonizing tendencies. They grow chained together in groups, often on the plants or sides of the aquarium.

Worms, Leaches, and Planaria

What we call worms are actually many different animals from several major unrelated groups that share a similar body shape.

Snails may become a nuisance in your aquatic garden.

A worm often found as food for the aquarium fish are tubifex.
These worms can also live in the aquarium, if the fish don't get them all. They are sold frozen, freeze dried, and in flakes. You can also sometimes get live tubifex worms for your fish.

Tubifex worms are true worms and related to earthworms. They are very small and live on the bottom in small tubes. They live head down and wave their tales out of the tubes, sifting mud while looking for food. They are often found naturally in dirty areas.

Tubifex worms have been suggested as possible carriers of disease and parasites, and other invertebrates can come in with live tubifex worms. These should be considered when feeding live foods of any kind. They can be very beneficial to fish but also have possible downsides too, so you should consider whether you want to use them or not. Prepared worms, frozen, freeze dried, or flake should all be safe.

Leeches and planaria are different types of worms that may be found in the aquarium. Though leeches can get into the aquarium it's much more likely if you see something that looks like a leech, it is probably planaria.

Leeches are most well known for their blood sucking. Different types of leeches attack different animals, and some even eat plants or dead animals.

Planaria are much more likely to be found in the aquarium where they can reproduce and thrive. They are usually white or light tan. They can be differentiated from the leeches by their shape. Planaria have heads that have hornlike growths on the sides of their heads and visual eye spots.

Planaria can do very well in the aquarium. They are hermaphroditic and can reproduce both sexual and asexually. Asexually they can split in the middle creating two planaria from one. Sexually they can serve as either the male or female, but cannot fertilize their own eggs. As you can see it makes it very easy for them to be prolific in the aquarium. They are difficult to get rid of, though some gouramis may eat them.

More Arthropods in Your Fish Tank

We've already looked at one arthropod, the shrimp. Crustaceans will be the most likely type of arthropods in your aquarium, but sometimes you may encounter insects, or very rarely spiders.

Athropods

There are over a million discovered species of arthropods, about 80 percent of the earth's total. The most distinguishing characteristic of this group is their segmented exoskeleton. They have hard protective outer armor. Arthropods have well developed systems and complicated sensory organs like antennae and eyes.

There are many small crustaceans that may come in to your home aquarium. Some can hitchhike in on plants, others are introduced as a live foods. Some of those that may be encountered include clam shrimp, cyclops, *Daphnia,* and *Gammarus.*

Clam shrimp and cyclops are more likely to just show up in your tank, though sometimes cyclops species are cultured as live foods. These are both small animals and you really have to be looking for them to see them. Clam shrimp look like tiny swimming clams and cyclops look like tiny little tops with arms. These animals are not harmful to your fish and will probably be eaten happily.

Daphnia are common small animals found in water and puddles all over. There are similar related animals that all get clumped in the same group. These generally look like small dots swimming in the water. They can be orange, green, tan, or brown.

Daphnia are a well favored fish food for many small and medium sized fish. They are also usually relatively easy to culture for a regular supply of live fish food. They will usually do very well if kept in a bucket of green water.

Insects

You don't usually get too many insects in the home aquarium, though you may see plenty in a home pond. They will occasionally come into your aquarium on plants. Though there are several full time aquatic insects, many only spend the first part of their lives in the water. If you have an uncovered tank without fish you may be surprised by the number of insect larva that can show up.

Dragonflies are pretty insects, but you don't want their young around your fishes.

Insects should not generally be kept with fish, unless one is meant as food for the other. You can feed some insects to some fish, and some fish to some insects.

Many insects fly, even the aquatic ones. If you decide to try keeping aquatic insects as a hobby, they need to have covered tanks, or you could end up with them anywhere.

True Bugs

Alright I'll admit that bugs aren't for everyone, but they can be really interesting to study and the kids usually love them.

Some of the most commonly seen water bugs are the water boatmen, back swimmers, and water skaters. If you ever spent time playing in healthy natural waters you have probably seen at least one of these bugs.

Water boatmen and back swimmers are similar in appearance. The most obvious difference is that the water boatman swims right side up, while the back swimmer swims upside down. Water boatmen form the largest family of water bugs and are found all over the world. In their diet the water boatman eats mostly plants and debris while the back swimmer is predacious. Back swimmers have toxic saliva and can eat animals larger than themselves; they can also deliver a painful bite.

Part 5

Water skaters, pond skaters, water striders, water treaders, and water measurers are all names for a similar group of predacious bugs. These slender bugs have long legs used to skate across the water surface. They hold victims with their front legs as they feed on them.

You hopefully won't ever find giant water bugs or water scorpions in your aquarium accidentally, though they are rather interesting as pets. If you're collecting your own live foods, these are some true bugs you might want to watch out for. The giant water bug is very large, up to 4 inches that can not only swim but fly too. They are predators that can also bite humans. Water scorpions look somewhat like a walking stick. I think they're a very interesting as a single small tank inhabitant. They will eat mosquito larva and other small live foods.

Beetles

There aren't a lot of aquatic beetles but they can be interesting if you happen to come across one. Most beetles are terrestrial, but a few of them live on or under the water surface. Many aquatic beetles spend time out of the water too. Most of them are good fliers. If you happen to keep them, be sure to cover the tank or you may find them elsewhere in other tanks or around the house.

Some of the aquatic beetles can be rather colorful, with bright oranges or yellows, pretty blues and greens, stripes or spots, though most are brown or black. Beetles rarely come in on plants, though sometimes their larva may. Beetles are often available in natural waters. Some beetles are scavengers but others are predators and will not work well with your fish. It's best to keep this sort of project in separate tanks.

Flies

You might not think of flies in the water but there are a lot of flies and many of them spend their youths as aquatics. A young fly is called larva. Black flies, crane flies, gnats, some horseflies, hover flies, midges, mosquitoes, and no-see-ums are some of the flies with aquatic larva. Larvae look kind of like worms though some have more obvious heads and other parts. Larval stages can vary in length lasting from a few weeks to several years. Adult flies are not aquatic.

The fly larvae you are most likely to encounter are generally used as live foods and include the larva of gnats, midges, and mosquitoes. The most well-known of these to hobbyists is the mosquito. There are more than 1600 kinds of mosquito worldwide, some of which can transmit fatal diseases to humans. Not all mosquitoes transmit disease, the majority don't. Just some particular species can transmit some particular diseases. Only female mosquitoes bite.

Female mosquitoes lay their eggs in floating bunches, called rafts, on just about any water surface. The mosquito larva and pupae are aquatic. These are relished as live foods by most aquariums fish. They are usually easy to find in most standing bodies of water, if you have ditches, ponds, or long-standing puddles in your area, you are likely to find mosquito larva in it.

> ### Live Foods:
> ### to feed or not to feed?
>
> There is some debate on the safety of live foods if the risk of possibly introducing an outside organism is worth the benefit of live natural foods. Aquarists have to decide for themselves where they feel comfortable with on this issue. The type of tank, the fish being kept in it, if they are breeding, and whether contaminants might attack eggs or fry, all should be considered when deciding whether or not to feed live foods.

Another fly larva often found for sale as fish food, live, frozen, freeze dried in flakes or pellets, and probably several other ways, are midge larva, called bloodworms. This larva can often be found in just about any water that's been standing for any length of time. Blood worms live in a tube in the mud and debris on the bottom. If rinsed off, the red worms are very visible. Some people have allergies to these worms, so care should be taken when using them.

The final fly larva that's sometimes found for the aquarium fish are the glassworms. These are the larva of a type of gnat. They are rather interesting clear worm like animals that float in the cold northern waters in the winter.

Remember when feeding live foods that any of these larva can turn into adult flies if they aren't eaten. It's not really a good thing to have them flying around your house biting people, and other family members may not be sympathetic. Be sure to only feed enough live foods to your fish that can be eaten rapidly.

Dragonflies, Damselflies, and More Flies
Dragonflies and the smaller damselflies are attractive insects often depicted in art. These

insects lay their eggs in the water and the nymphs (baby dragonflies and damselflies) are aquatic, eventually developing into the colorful adults. It's very surprising how many flies spend their childhoods in the water.

Occasionally a dragonfly or damselfly larva will find its way into the home aquarium. These are rather large insects. The dragonfly nymphs are usually larger than damselfly nymphs. The damselfly nymphs also have unusual gills. Their gills look like three feathery tails at the end of its body. These are not on dragonfly nymphs.

Both young and adult dragonflies and damselflies are predators. This is great if you want to eradicate mosquitoes in your area, which they do prey on, but it can be a terrible disaster in your aquarium. The nymphs are good at hiding among plants and picking small fish off one at a time. If you see one of these critters in your tank, remove it.

Other common flies whose nymphs live in the water include mayflies, stoneflies, and caddisflies. These flies are all well known to fly fishermen. Caddisfly nymphs are particularly interesting and build themselves little houses of twigs, stones, or other available materials.

Part Six
Plants and More Plants

Plant? And Not

Whose Kingdom?

When scientists first started dividing organisms into kingdoms, there were two: Plant and Animal. Even though they were aware of organisms that are now in the other kingdoms before that time, they had been classified in one of those two until 1969, when the five kingdoms system was initiated.

The five kingdoms include Monera, Protista, Plantae, Fungi, and Animalia. Monera is the kingdom of the prokaryotes. These have a different kind of cell than other organisms; they include bacteria and the dreaded blue-green algae, cyanobacteria. The other four kingdoms all have the same cell type and are called eukaryotes. The

Aquatic plants come in a wide assortment of shapes, sizes, and colors.

kingdom of Protista is basically the tiny things that don't fit in the other kingdoms; algae are included in this kingdom. Plantae includes, among others, ferns and flowers, bushes, and trees. Animalia includes insects, fish, reptiles, mammals, birds, and more. Fungi are generally decomposers and include mushrooms and toadstools.

There are photosynthesizing organisms in three of the kingdoms, and all of them have visible members that are relevant in some way to the planted aquarium. Not everything that's green is really a plant.

The Kingdom Monera

The kingdom of Monera is the kingdom of the prokaryotes, the first organisms to develop on the earth. These single-celled organisms are often referred to as bacteria, and live everywhere on the planet that life is possible, including places where eukaryotes can't survive.

Bacteria are single celled but can form groups or colonies. They reproduce asexually by cell division. This means they tend to double every reproductive cycle. For some bacteria, this can be as quick as 20 minutes. In 20 minutes, 1 would go to 2; in 40 minutes, there would be 4; then 8 in an hour; 64 in 2 hours; and 512 in 3 hours. The colony would reach a million in less than 7 hours.

Blue-green algae can cover the entire aquarium.

Blue-Green Algae

Cyanobacteria are neither plants nor algae; they are photosynthetic nitrogen-fixing bacteria from the kingdom of Monera. These prokaryotes are believed to have developed during the earlier periods of life on earth when the nutrients they were absorbing in the primordial seas began to be used up. Eventually, some of these developed to use water and carbon dioxide to photosynthesize. These are the cyanobacteria, one of the first real oxygen producers.

Most bacteria are helpful; in fact, they're essential to life for humans and all eukaryotes. As you read earlier, they're what make it possible to have an aquarium at all. But not all bacteria are good in all places, and slimy coatings of stinky blue-green algae are not what most people want in their lovely underwater gardens.

Cyanobacteria are usually dark blue-green (hence the name), but can be other shades, including gray and brown. Most cyanobacteria are in fresh water, but there are also some in other wet places like the seas, damp soils, and mulm. Some have formed a symbiotic relationship with fungus to create lichens. Cyanobacteria can be singular, in groups, or colonizing. The ones most often noticed in the aquarium form colonies of sheets that are slimy to the touch and have a peculiar odor. In the aquarium, cyanobacteria will often coat the plants, decorations, and gravel. Left untreated, the heavy coats of cyanobacteria can smother and kill your plants.

Some methods for removing cyanobacteria are manual removal, increased oxygen and water flow, strict limiting of lighting to no more than eight hours a day, and the medication erythromycin. Extra water changes can't hurt, and if not a total cure-all, they at least help alleviate many aquarium ailments.

Protista: What's in the Pond Water?

The kingdom of Protista is a diverse kingdom that includes the first eukaryotes. Protists need water and live in fresh and sea water, with some in moist soils and mulm. They also live in wet hosts in both symbiotic and parasitic relationships. All protists can reproduce asexually; some can also do so sexually. Most are aerobic, breathing oxygen. If they are plant-like, they're usually called algae; if they're animal-like, they are called protozoa; or if they're fungus-like they are called slime molds.

Hair algae is another annoyance that can cover everything in your tank.

Medications

Check your local fish or pet shop for medications to cure bacterial infections. Look for medications with erythromycin as a main ingredient, then treat as directed by the manufacturer. This may interfere with the biological filters in your tank; remember, the good bacteria mentioned back in the nitrogen cycle section. You'll also have waste from the cyanobacteria you've killed off, so be sure to do a water change before and after each treatment, and plan to continue to do several water changes after the final treatment has ended.

Protists are mostly tiny single-celled organisms, but large seaweeds are also included. Originally, only unicellular organisms were included in this kingdom, but later research disclosed that some "plants" were more closely related to some of the algae.

The Many Faces of Algae

Algae can refer to a wide range of photosynthesizing organisms. These range in size from tiny floating single cells to giant seaweeds like kelp, though some biologists believe the larger algae should still be classified as plants. And like cyanobacteria, some algae have formed symbiotic relationships with fungus to create lichens.

Seven phyla are often considered algae. Those include Bacillariophyta, Chlorophyta, Chrysophyta, Dinoflagellata, Euglenophyta, Phaeophyta, and Rhodophyta. Most of the over 21,000 species of organisms represented as algae are unicellular.

Bacillariophyta are also called diatoms. They are often brown and live in both fresh and salt water, many in plankton. Diatomaceous earth is fossilized diatoms. These can show up in your aquarium as a brown scum on the inside surfaces of the tank.

Red algae will encrust wood and rocks.

Chlorophyta are green algae, and are most commonly encountered in the aquarium. They're most commonly found in fresh water, but many live in salt water. There are over 7,000 species of green algae, and they can live in diverse places—such as floating as plankton and in symbiotic relationships with anemones and fungus.

In the aquarium, green algae encountered include green water, floating unicellular algae, slimy algae on the glass, and colonizing algae encrusting the decorations, plants, and gravel. Algae living in long colonies produce the much-dreaded hair algae. Green algae can also be multicellular and form macroalgae like caulerpa, which is sometimes used in reef aquariums.

Chrysophyta are also called golden algae. They are often colonial and live among freshwater plankton.

Dinoflagellata are in both fresh and marine waters and are commonly called dinoflagellates. These algae spin as they swim. Explosive population blooms of dinoflagellates cause red tides.

Euglenophyta are euglena and related organisms; they are green and usually live in fresh water. Euglena is most often found in murky, nasty pond water.

Phaeophyta are brown algae, all of which are multicellular; these are found in marine waters and include the giant seaweeds like kelp.

Rhodophyta are red algae and are represented in the planted aquarium by black beard algae. Most red algae are multicellular and occur in salt water, but some are in fresh water as well.

And What About Plants?

Generally, plants are multicellular photosynthesizing eukaryotes–there's a mouthful. A few algae also fit that description, and some believe they should also be considered as plants. This is another area where even the experts can't agree.

Algae in the Aquarium

In the aquarium, an almost unlimited number of algae can show up. Some of them actually look nice and are even being sold now (for example, as algae balls). But plenty of algae can show up unwelcome, and you won't want them to stay in your aquarium.

Generally, causes of an overgrowth of algae include too much light or too many nutrients. To help combat these problems, check for unwanted sunlight reaching the aquarium, and limit lighting hours to eight to ten a day. Be sure to keep up on water changes, and check filters if appropriate. Planting more plants, especially fast-growing plants and floating plants, to help block light can be of help. Several fish, shrimp, and snails are also effective in eating different types of algae, as mentioned in the chapter on fishes and invertebrates.

And finally, if you get a bad algae growth, it may just be bad luck, so don't be too hard on yourself. Just try to keep it out manually. Keep working on getting a full tank of plants, and eventually it should wear itself out. It's not unusual or necessarily bad to have a small bit of algae in your tank; after all, it is very natural.

Photosynthesis

There's a common thought that plants breathe in carbon dioxide (CO_2) and release oxygen (O_2), but this isn't exactly true. Plant cells, like most eukaryotes, are aerobic, and use O_2 and release CO_2. But plants do something else, too: they photosynthesize. Photosynthesizing is using the energy of light to create compounds from CO_2 and water (H_2O).

For example:

$$6CO_2 + 6H_2O = C_6H_{12}O_6 + 6O_2$$

What this means is that six carbon dioxide and six water molecules were converted to one sugar and six oxygen molecules, which were then released. This is done with a special pigment called chlorophyll. It's the ability of plants to create these sugars that make them great food for the rest of the organisms, and their waste product, oxygen, lets us all breathe.

Almost all plants reproduce sexually, but most also reproduce by asexual propagation, which is certainly the most common method among aquarium plants.

Lichens are a symbiotic relationship between fungus and algae or cyanobacteria.

Plants photosynthesize and produce oxygen when they're receiving the correct amount of light. Plants only photosynthesize while in the light, but in a normal day, they produce more oxygen in the hours they're photosynthesizing than they use around the clock while respiring. The oxygen they release are those little bubbles you can see on the plants and algae in your aquarium. In water, that oxygen generally tries to escape, and doesn't just sit in the tank at night when the lights are out.

The first and most primitive plants are called bryophytes. These include the mosses, liverworts, and hornworts (which are not the same as the floating aquarium plant also called hornwort, *Ceratophyllum demersum*, which is an angiosperm). The bryophytes probably aren't closely related, but they are all primitive plants without root systems. They can have rootlike holds called rhizoids, but those don't function as roots do.

The pteridophytes (meaning "feather plants") developed later. These plants are seedless and include horsetails, club mosses, and ferns. Horsetails are often used in ponds, but of these three plants, only ferns are generally used in the home aquarium. There are several lovely aquatic ferns. Mosses and ferns reproduce sexually to create spores, which are less advanced than seeds.

The first seeded plants were gymnosperms. These include plants like ginkgos and conifers, which produce cones. The gymnosperms have a less-developed seed than the angiosperms, which have enclosed seeds.

Finally, the flowering plants, or angiosperms, came with enclosed seeds. This gave them a great advantage over the other plants, and now they are the most prevalent plants on the planet. Most aquarium plants are angiosperms. Vegetables, fruits, maple trees, willows, grasses, tulips, orchids, and roses are all angiosperms.

Freshwater aquatic plants are believed to have originally developed from plants that had come onto the land and adapted to it, then went back into the water. For simplicity's sake, I'll group the plants in chapters based on their basic type of growth.

Also, be aware that some aquarium plants have been declared invasive, and different laws may exist concerning plants in your state. I've tried to mention some of the plants that I know there are issues with, but it's not possible for me to be aware of all federal

Horsetails are a primitive plant often found in wet environments.

Flowering plants are called angiosperms.

Some plants have been
declared invasive.

and local laws concerning all plants, and they change with time. This is also true of fish and other animals. If there is some concern, you will have to check on your own local laws.

Floating Plants

Floating plants are those that float on the top of the water and don't generally take root in the substrate. Some of these plants take up nutrients out of the water through their leaves and stems, though some also form floating roots. Some are totally submersed, while others form leaves above the water.

Floating plants can be useful in many ways. They can provide extra cover for protecting fish, help in fish breeding, provide shade for the tank, and help clean up excess nutrients in the water.

Floating plants can work quite well for giving fish refuge from their tankmates. You may want to give fish some extra plants if you are adding

Floating plants can accent your aquatic garden nicely.

new fish, to provide cover for different species in a mixed tank. Floating plants are also quite helpful in breeding fish, providing cover for females during spawning or cover for young fry from the parents. Some labyrinth fish even include small floating plants in their nests.

Adding floating plants to your tank can also be useful in lowering the amount of light that gets to the bottom of a tank. And some aquarists like to use them to remove excess nutrients from the tank. Many of these plants are also used in biological sewage treatment.

Planting floating plants is very easy: just put them in the water. Trimming and reproduction will depend on the type of plants. Some float under the surface, and some have leaves above the water, with roots floating below. Some plants can be floating plants but can also grow roots, like water ferns, or are used as a ground cover like *Riccia*; these are covered in a later chapter. If your floating plants block too much light from the rest of the tank, just scoop them out.

Hornwort

Hornwort is a common plant with distribution in many places throughout the world. It grows on long stems with whorls of needle-like, stiff, branching leaves–the "horns." Though there has been debate over the number of species, currently the common belief is that there are two, *Ceratophyllum demersum* and *C. submersum*. All hornworts are very similar in appearance, though they differ in the number of horns on the leaves and in their length, with *C. submersum* coming out ahead on both counts.

Hornwort is a floating plant that doesn't form roots.

Hornworts can flower and produce seeds, but the flowers and seeds are small and inconspicuous. The plant usually has vegetative reproduction; it just keeps growing, and parts of the stem break off, and then they keep growing. The easiest way to get more hornwort plants growing at home is the same way: snip or pinch the stems apart. The pieces will just keep growing, creating another plant.

The species of hornwort most often found in the aquarium hobby is *C. demersum*. Depending on the conditions it's grown under, it can vary in color from several shades of green in lower lighting to yellows, reds, and pinks in higher light levels.

Hornwort is unusual in that it grows no roots. Even though it is often found at pet stores with an anchor holding it down, it shouldn't be planted. Planted stems will die off at the bottom and end up floating anyway. Some hobbyists will continually reanchor these plants down to keep them as stemmed plants; they can look attractive in this way, but there are several stemmed plants that look very similar to hornwort that do root naturally and might be easier to use in this application.

Hornwort is an excellent aquarium plant. It grows well in conditions where many other plants may fail. It does well in hard water, generally preferring it, and does fine in lower to medium light levels. And it can grow rapidly, sometimes needing to be regularly thinned. It's generally considered a cool water plant, but my tanks run quite warm, and I grow hornwort in several of them.

Hornwort is a classical aquarium plant. It looks lovely hanging down over a tank, and makes a great cover for fry and other small or timid top-water fish. It's particularly useful in breeding livebearers. Hornwort is also used to help clean water and is considered a good oxygenator.

Duckweed and *Wolffia*

Lemna (duckweeds), *Spirodela* (giant duckweeds), and *Wolffia* are similar in appearance but different in size; *Spirodela* is the largest and *Wolffia* are the smallest. Duckweeds are generally distributed worldwide. These are small plants that usually have tiny green leaves that float on the surface of the water. The rootlike structure can become very long and hang underneath the plant. *Wolffia* has tiny leaves and looks like little dots of green floating at the top of the water.

Here, duckweed is found growing in a puddle next to a creek.

These are some of the smallest flowering plants, yet

flowering and seeds are not the main form of reproduction in these plants; in fact, they're rather uncommon. These plants usually use vegetative reproduction. Each floating leaf can produce more floating leaves.

Duckweed is an interesting plant. You can probably find it at a local pond, and more than likely, there will be several species growing together. It grows incredibly fast and can become an unsightly nuisance, but it also has special abilities that make it useful in the treatment of wastewater. Duckweed also contains more protein and other nutrients than most other plants, making it a good candidate for animal and poultry feed and as a fertilizer.

Though duckweed may help clean up your tank water, this isn't generally a good plant for a planted tank. It will grow so thickly on the top of a tank that it cuts out light for any other plants trying to grow below. It can also drop roots all over the bottom of the tank, making an unsightly mess. Duckweed will also cling to everything, like the sides of your tanks, and your arm, if you put it in the tank. If you like duckweed and want to have some in your tank, it will most likely grow very well for you, but you will have to be willing to thin it regularly.

There are many types of floating plants that can be used in Your aquatic garden.

Wolffia is a more popular choice for aquariums, if it's available. It does have a couple of drawbacks. *Wolffia* is a nice food for many fish, and often will get eaten up in the aquarium.

Spirodela are similar plants, but they are larger and not seen as often in the aquarium trade. They are sometimes found for ponds.

Riccia

Yes, *Riccia* is really a floating plant, but due to the recent popularity, it's been given as a tied-down bottom plant, and because it's a liverwort, we put it in Chapter 22 with the ferns and mosses.

Salvinia and Azolla

Salvinia and *Azolla* are generally attractive floating ferns, but often have the potential to do a great deal of damage to ecosystems that they invade. The exact relationship between the two types of plants is somewhat in debate: *Azolla* are sometimes put into the same family as *Salvinia* and sometimes placed in a family of their own. Several of these plants can cause ecological damage when they are introduced either intentionally or accidentally into non-native environments.

There are several types of *Salvinia*. They originate in various tropical locations; several come from Brazil, including the one that causes the most trouble, *S. molesta*. These plants grow well in ponds but are out of control in the wild, where they can reproduce at an incredible rate, creating huge mats of floating plants. The Federal Noxious Weed List includes *Salvinia* species. Though these are attractive plants and some may grow in the aquarium, they should not be recommended because of the ecological damage they may cause.

Azolla is a small, attractive floating fern. It seems to prefer going through seasonal changes and at times can become very red in color. It generally does better in a pond than an aquarium.

There are several species of *Azolla* in different locations, but some have become invasive in areas that they aren't native to. *A. pinnata* is native to waters in Africa, Asia, and Australia, but has gotten into waters in North America and elsewhere, where it has become a noxious weed, and is listed as such on the US Federal List. Adding to the confusion is its similarity in appearance to the North American native *A. caroliniana*.

Water Hyacinth, Water Lettuce, and Frogbit

Three other plants that are sometimes available are water lettuce (*Pistia stratiotes*), water hyacinth (*Eichhornia crassipes*), and frogbit (*Limnobium* spp). These plants

Out of control!

When out of control in non-native areas, *Azolla* can be a problem, but it also has a good side. *Azolla* has an interesting symbiotic relationship with a type of cyanobacteria (blue-green algae). The cyanobacteria have nitrogen-fixation abilities, similar to legumes. Because they are easy to grow in a marshy environment, they are easy to grow in rice paddies, and are used as an important green manure for rice production. *Azolla* can also be used as food for fish or other livestock, and can even be eaten by humans.

Water hyacinth is a popular and prolific floating plant.

generally tend to fare better in ponds than in aquariums. All float on the top of the water and send fairly large roots to the bottom of the tank.

Eichhornia crassipes (often called water hyacinth) is an attractive plant that is native to South America and is often used in ponds. It floats on top of the water and has unusual, pretty, green leaves. It flowers easily and has attractive violet flowers. Unfortunately, this plant can also cause a lot of problems when it gets into waters where it doesn't naturally occur, and it is legally controlled in some states.

Pistia stratiotes is also called water lettuce because of it's appearance–it looks like a floating head of lettuce. This is another rather common pond plant. Like water hyacinth, it can form dense mats of vegetation in water, causing problems for boating and water flow.

Limnobium (called frogbit) looks a lot like very large duckweed. Unlike the two plants above, the leaves generally float on the water instead of coming far out over it, which makes this plant more practical for the aquarium. It is an attractive plant, though it may be easier to grow outside in a pond than in the aquarium.

Stemmed Plants

Now we're ready to start having some real fun. Stemmed plants are most likely going to make up a large part of your underwater garden. They come in a wonderful variety of leaf types, shapes, and colors, including some striking reds and purples.

Many stemmed plants grow fast and are easy to care for; with many of these plants, you'll soon be wondering what to do with all your trimmings. However, there are also some that are harder to grow and have high lighting requirements. This guide will help you choose the right stemmed plants for your aquarium.

Now we're ready to start having some real fun!

Planting Stemmed Plants

When you buy your stemmed plants, they will usually be sold in bunches. These are held together with a rubber band or lead weight, which should be removed. The rubber band or weight will pinch the stems and usually kill that portion of the plant.

> ### Options for Extras
>
> And what do you do with all those extra plants you'll soon have? Here are some options:
>
> • Check with your local fish store. Many will accept plants in trade for store credit on live-stock.
>
> • Go to a local aquarium club meeting. Most have auctions where you can buy and sell fish and plants.
>
> • Trade with other aquarists. Swap for different plants or a new fish.

After removing the rubber band or weight, inspect your plants. Remove any dead, dried, or crushed portions. These will just decay further in the aquarium and threaten the healthy portions of your plants. Common scissors are good for this. You can pinch portions off with your fingers if you can do it without crushing the healthy portion of the plant; long fingernails are helpful here.

The best way to plant the stemmed plants is to have enough gravel in your tank to hold the plants down. Your gravel, or chosen substrate, should be at least 2 to 3 inches thick. This will be thick enough so the stems can be placed far enough into the substrate to hold them down.

Place the stems singly or in small groups; you'll have to take into account how large the plant leaves are when deciding. With a smaller-leafed plant, like *Rotala indica*, you can put two or three stems together and plant clusters of small groups. With a larger-leafed plant such as *Hygrophilia difformis*, stems should be planted a few inches apart. Otherwise, the large leaves on one plant will shade the leaves of plants around it, killing them.

When planting, use one or two fingers to support the stem while you put it in the gravel. Start an inch or two from where you want the stem to be. Holding the stem, put your fingers on the surface of the gravel and push into it in a downward arch. Stop when you get to the bottom and bring your fingers up slowly, leaving the stem behind in the gravel. Gently push some of the surrounding gravel around the stem, evening out the area. Continue planting each stem or group of stems until you're done.

Whether you're planting or trimming a stemmed plant, be aware that the most important part of the plant is the node–the part where the leaf of the plant connects to the stem, and the place where roots and new stems grow from. The spaces of stem in between nodes are fine to cut, though you should leave a small portion of the stem on the sides of the node. If you get too close, it will sometimes kill the node. At least one node needs to be under the gravel, though I would recommend two or three for most plants. Also be sure to remove any leaves that will be below the gravel, since they will just rot underground.

You should also have several nodes above the gravel; I would recommend keeping more nodes above the gravel for a stemmed plant that isn't established, though when trimming an established plant, you should be able to trim down to the last few nodes above the gravel. The number of nodes you use above or below the gravel will also depend on the plant. Some have much more space between nodes than others, so use common sense.

Trimming

Stemmed plants do need to be trimmed regularly. Without trimming, your underwater garden will soon be nothing more than an underwater mess. You'll have lots of plants floating at the top and absolutely nothing underneath.

There are two schools of thought on the best way to trim stemmed plants. One recommended course of action is to pull the plants out, trim off the bottoms, and then replant the tops. The other method is to trim the plants near the bottom. The tops can then be replanted to make new plants, either in the same or other aquariums.

Pulling and replanting does keep the plants looking nicer more often, since you never see the clipped bottoms. It does have a possible disadvantage, since mulm may come up in the water and make a mess when the roots are pulled up.

Growing Plants

When you start growing plants in your aquatic garden, begin with plants that have a good chance of actually growing—those that are considered easy plants. Many plants that are commonly sold don't have a very good chance of surviving in the average aquarium. Begin with plants that will tolerate a wide range of water and lighting conditions.

Trimming and leaving the bottoms of the plant will produce bushy plants, doesn't disturb the gravel, and is a little easier, but the trimmed plants will show while they grow out again. This is my favorite way to keep plants trimmed. It's somewhat less work; if you just do a couple stems every week or so, it usually stays fairly nice, and you don't notice the trimmings.

Alternanthera reineckii

This beautiful plant originates from South America. It's naturally red to purple on the underside of the leaves, and this natural tendency has been used to cultivate various shades of pink, red, purple, and green. The leaves are also variable in shape. *A. reineckii* will stay small enough to use in the mid to foreground of your aquarium if you give it adequate lighting, but can grow leggy if not given enough light, though it will more likely just die.

This is often a difficult plant to grow because it needs a lot of light to stay alive. It will also probably need supplemental nutrients. They are usually grown emersed before arriving at your local fish store. After being put into your tank, they will probably lose their leaves. New leaves and roots will grow from the nodes where the old leaves had been. If you can successfully grow these plants, they are very attractive.

Bacopa caroliniana and *B. monnireri*

Bacopa, also called water hyssop, is an easily grown plant that adapts to many conditions. You can trim it regularly and keep it fairly short, let it grow taller as a background plant, or let it grow right out of your tank, where it may even flower.

There are several types of *Bacopa*, but the most commonly found available for home aquariums are *Bacopa caroliniana* and *B. monnireri*. These two plants have round, rubbery leaves. The leaves of *B. caroliniana* are darker and have a rounded point at the tip, while those of *B. monnireri* are lighter green, oval, and

Bacopa likes to grow out of the tank to flower.

Bacopa

Bacopa is an herb, and broken pieces are aromatic. Some people eat it, even tossing it on salads. *B. monnireri* is claimed to aid in functions of the mind and some of the ailments that affect it, like epilepsy and Alzheimer's, and generally benefit performance overall. It's also been claimed to be calming.

smaller. *B. caroliniana*'s flower is violet or blue and can be dark; *B. monnireri* has a whiter flower, sometimes with a faint tinting of violet, pink, or blue in the middle.

B. monnireri is distributed in many tropical and subtropical areas throughout the world, while *B. caroliniana* is a North American native. Both types can grow in some areas of North America.

There are other very decorative types of *Bacopa* native to South America that are rarely available in the aquarium trade in the United States.

These plants can grow very well in the home aquarium. *Bacopa* is a bog plant and prefers to grow with roots wet and stems out of the water, but it will grow well underwater if regularly trimmed. Plant stems individually in group clusters. It can look nice as a foreground plant if you trim it regularly and keep it short, or longer for farther back in the tank. If you let it grow out of your tanks, it will happily grow into any adjoining tanks, which mine does regularly. *Bacopa* can also grow well in paludariums and outside in ponds.

Cabomba

Cabomba is a lovely fragile plant native to warmer parts of the Americas. These plants are also called fanwort, and have been used in aquariums for years. *C. caroliniana* is native to the southern United States and so is very available for harvest and sale. Even though it has been offered for long time and is usually readily available at local stores, *Cabomba* can be difficult to maintain, particularly for the long term.

There are several different species and varieties offered, and colors range from silvery green to green to brown and red. Cabombas prefer very clean water, and do better in softer water. They also need high light levels. Some *Cabomba* may be easier to maintain in your water conditions than others; if you have trouble with one type, another may succeed.

Cabomba can be fragile in the aquarium.

Part 6

Plants look nice if stems are planted individually in groups. Some *Cabomba* will form floating leaves at the water surface in addition to the lacy leaves formed under the water. These leaves are oval and are similar in appearance to some of the water lily leaves.

You should also check your local laws concerning *Cabomba* in your state, since it has been introduced in some areas where it's caused problems. Though not on the Federal Noxious Weed List, it may be illegal in your area.

Didiplis diandra

This is a unique-looking North American native plant with long thin leaves. It is highly sought-after for the planted aquarium. *D. diandra* is also called water hedge. It likes high lighting in clean water and is difficult to grow.

When it is growing well, this plant can get pinkish shades in the upper leaves. Plant individual stems far enough apart so the leaves of one stem won't shade its neighbor, and treat the stems gently, as they are easily damaged.

This is another plant that will not take algae infestations well. This is a more difficult plant, but if you can get it to grow, it will make a dramatic focal point in the aquarium.

Egeria densa

Commonly called anacharis, this is an old standard in aquarium and pond plants. This was the early standard for the goldfish bowl. *Egeria densa* is cultivated in tanks and ponds and has been introduced into natural bodies of water throughout much of the world.

Anacharis has been said to dislike high temperatures, but some plants will do fine into the mid-80s for several months. Different populations seem to be able to deal with different conditions.

Even though this is a common aquarium plant, it can sometimes be difficult to grow. Anacharis likes good

Egeria najas is a more attractive relative of the well-known anacharis group.

lighting and can be grown well in filtered window light, which is one of the reasons it was so popular with goldfish bowls in the past. More than likely, the plants outlived the majority of the goldfish.

A smaller related plant, *E. najas*, is sometime available. This one needs very good lighting, even more so than *E. densa* does. *E. najas* is an attractive plant and is worth growing if you can find it.

When you plant anacharis in your tank, be sure to separate the stems and plant each one individually. As your anacharis grows, you will probably notice that the new growth doesn't look like the plant you bought. It will probably be lighter green, less dense, and the leaves will be more curled. This is because the anacharis you bought was grown in ponds where it got a lot more light than it will get in your aquarium.

Glossostigma elatinoides

The discus of the plant world, these little plants are from Australia and surrounding areas. Often just called *Glossostigma*, this is probably one of the more difficult and most sought-after aquarium plants. These plants are tiny, and when growing well, will cover the aquarium floor with a carpet of little green leaves.

These plants are usually purchased in small pots or mats, though one of the biggest problems is acquiring the plant in good health to begin with. This plant ships very poorly and fades fast if it doesn't like the conditions it's kept in. Try to get these plants as soon as possible after they're delivered to your local fish store, and if they don't look healthy, don't bother. If you order these through the mail, you may want to request they be shipped in water, as sometimes this can help those plants that ship poorly.

These plants are grown emersed for the aquarium trade, and the growth pattern will change once you get them growing in your tanks. This plant requires high lighting in a clean tank. When you plant *Glossostigma*, take small, pinch-sized portions of the plant and insert into the substrate. You can plant these in clusters, but leave a small space between them. It's likely that a few of the tiny plants will not survive, and by planting them in these small groups, it will help ensure that rot won't spread and kill large numbers of your little plants. The space will also help keep them clean, let in more light, and give them some space to start growing.

Once your *Glossostigma* starts to grow, it will spread across the substrate in rows of tiny pairs of leaves. These should spread over the aquarium bottom wherever they can get enough light. Once you get this plant growing, it does very nicely and looks impressive.

Gymnocoronis spilanthoides

A South American plant, *G. spilanthoides* is a larger-leafed stemmed plant. These plants like to grow out of the tank, and with their fast growth, they can do so very quickly.

If you want to keep these plants emersed, you will have to keep them under strong lighting. Stems should be planted individually, with space between, and will need to be trimmed regularly.

If you're looking for plants that will grow right out of your tanks, these will do great, and can make a very interesting display grown that way. Just remember that either under or above the water, these are somewhat large plants that grow very quickly.

Hemianthus micranthemoides is not such a good choice for a carpeting plant.

Hemianthus micranthemoides

Previously called *Micranthemum micranthemoides*, this small-leafed plant can make a large bushy planting. These plants prefer moderate to high lighting. The stems can be planted in small groups and may develop runners, and in addition to growing upwards, may form runners across the gravel. Given reasonably good lighting, these are not difficult plants to grow.

You'll have to trim this plant regularly if you use it in the front of your tank; it tends to like to grow taller than foreground plants, and it can grow quickly. *H. micranthemoides* works well in the midground, and it can make a nice centerpiece or even background plant.

Heteranthera zosterifolia

This is a pretty, bright green plant with bunched, grassy stems. New bunches form on the branches at the nodes, with roots hanging down. *H. zosterifolia* comes from South America and is also called stargrass.

This plant usually looks better when kept shorter. Stargrass does need a lot of light to grow, and won't do well if attacked by algae. Plants should be planted individually or in very small groups.

Hydrocotyle

The pennyworts and their attractive leaves have long been favorites in the aquarium. These herbs are located throughout the world, and several are often offered for the aquarium.

Most of these plants grow on stems that grow up to the top, with a leaf and roots growing from the nodes. As an aquarium plant, they are very decorative and have a unique look.

> ### Pennyworts
>
> *Hydrocotyle verticillata* grows a bit differently than the other pennyworts. The stem grows like a runner along the substrate, and the leaves, which look like little umbrellas, grow up from the stem. The leaf stem can easily grow well over a foot to reach out of the top of a low tank. *H. verticillata* can also bloom regularly, sending a stem of puffball-like flowers out the top of your tank.

H. leucocephala is probably the most commonly found pennywort in the aquarium trade. It makes a nice feature plant in your aquarium and is usually planted in a small group. Other pennyworts are sometimes available; many need good lighting to show their best features in the tank. These plants will also grow very nicely emersed.

Hydrotriche hottoniiflora

This is a unique and attractive plant from Madagascar. The leaves somewhat resemble fir tree needles, but look most like prehistoric plants growing along waterways in paintings of dinosaurs. These plants aren't readily available but can sometimes be obtained from an aquarium-plant mail order business.

They like high lighting and will do poorly if infested with algae. Stems should be planted individually, but placed in groups.

Hygrophila

There are several popular aquarium plants from the genus *Hygrophila*. They can be grown under or above the water; the leaves on the same plant can

Hydrotriche hottoniiflora is a beautiful plant that needs excellent water and lighting to grow well.

look quite different depending on the medium. Some members of this genus can even be eaten.

Three species of *Hygrophila* from Asia are most commonly found in the local aquarium store. Many other species exist in Asia, Africa, and Australia; some of those are suitable for the aquarium, and some can occasionally be found for sale. Most need high lighting to grow successfully.

Hygrophila corymbosa

Commonly called giant hygro and sometimes listed as *Nomaphila corymbosa*, *Hygrophila corymbosa* is often available at local aquarium stores. These plants are usually grown emersed, and the leaves will usually fade away in the aquarium. The stems should be planted individually, with space between stems for the large leaves.

These plants require good lighting to grow well. Without it, the plant can last for quite a while, but tends to fade after time. These plants will grow better in a strongly lit aquarium with good filtration.

Hygrophila difformis

You're more likely to see this plant listed in your local fish store as water wisteria. It's a delicate-looking, lacy-leafed plant. The fern-like leaves are light green on the top and silvery on the bottom, and can be shaped differently depending on the conditions the plant is grown in. *H. difformis* doesn't look anything like the other *Hygrophila*.

These plants are lovely and can grow in relatively low to higher light levels. Not only are they versatile in their requirements, but they are also often found in pet stores. This plant is generally easy to grow.

Water wisteria is somewhat delicate when handled. Any portion of the plant wrapped in rubber bands or lead weights will most likely be bruised and will die. You're better off trimming off the end of the stem just past the last node.

Water wisteria can grow well even in low lighting.

When you plant your water wisteria, be sure to give each stem a large amount of space; they get big and will shade each other. Be gentle when you put the stems into the gravel, and be sure to plant the stem deeply so it won't come up. The more often you have to plant the water wisteria, the more likely you are to lose more of the stem.

Water wisteria is not fussy in its requirements. It does like a reasonably clean tank and doesn't tolerate algae well. When grown tall, it often loses the bottom leaves due to lack of light.

> ### New Roots
>
> An interesting thing about *Hygrophila difformis* is that a part of a leaf can turn into a whole plant. The leaf portions can start to grow roots and create a whole new plant. If parts of leaves break off and float to the surface, watch them and they may start to grow into new plants, too.

Water wisteria is a wonderful plant; I think it's one of the most attractive. Its unique look among aquarium plants and easy availability makes it a nice choice. It's a good plant for growing in the middle of a tank or in the front sides.

Hygrophila polysperma

H. polysperma is a long-used aquarium plant and is available in several colors. The problem with these plants is they are on the Federal Noxious Weed List in the United States and have caused trouble in other countries as well, so check local laws.

That being said, it is an attractive plant and is often readily available in pet stores. Several leaf shapes and colors have been produced from this plant, including one with a lot of red and yellow in it called "sunset hygro."

These plants, especially the cultivated colored varieties, do better with high lighting. *H. polysperma* stems should be planted singly or in small groups. It looks nice if the stems are planted close together to form a large group.

Limnophila

Limnophila are lacy-leafed plants from Asia, Africa, and Australia. These herbs are also commonly called ambulia. Several are often available for aquarists. Some of the *Limnophila* can be very similar in appearance and difficult for the novice to correctly identify.

L. aquatica is different than the others and is one of the most dramatic *Limnophila*, with wide, finely-divided leaves that give it the appearance of a giant green feather duster. The stems should be planted individually, rather far apart, and you'll need good lighting for this plant. It also won't do well with algae on its leaves.

Other species need similar care, with good lighting and individually planted stems, though they can be much closer depending on the length of the leaves. Other ambulia are usually planted in large clusters in the back of the aquarium.

L. sessifilora is another plant listed as a noxious weed. You should check local laws before obtaining this plant.

Ludwigia repens

This is a lovely plant native to North America. The leaves are purple on top and a pinkish shade on the bottom. The colors of *Ludwigia* can make a dramatic statement in your aquarium. When blooming, it has a small purple flower.

This plant is generally easy to grow. It does require good lighting, but if you supply that, the plant can grow very well. It isn't as fast-growing as some of the stemmed plants, but it is not a slow grower either. Stems should be planted individually. If you allow *Ludwigia* to grow to the top, the stems will spread out over the top of the tank, form different leaves, and form roots that it will send back down to the gravel. It should be trimmed regularly to avoid this.

Ludwigia is another of my favorites; it's an attractive plant, and certainly one of the easiest red-stemmed plants to grow. It makes a nice addition to the aquarium and should do well for you as long as you provide it with a little space and adequate lighting.

Ludwigia repens is an easy-to-grow species of red-leaved plant.

Lysimachia nummularia

This is a wonderful but underutilized plant. It's also sometimes called creeping Jenny or loosestrife. There are many loosestrife plants; several are used in flower gardens, but very few will survive life in water. *L. nummularia* can grow either under or above water, and is sometimes even used in gardens as a ground cover.

L. *nummularia* is an undemanding plant, though it does better in higher light levels. The leaves are small, round, and attractive, and are available in both green and yellow. Plant stems individually but close together. It can be kept trimmed relatively low, to grow in the mid-foreground, or you can let it grow taller for a background plant.

These plants are somewhat more difficult to find than some of the more common stemmed plants, but they are worth the trouble of locating. If you can't find these at a local aquarium store, they are available through some mail order businesses.

Mayaca fluviatilis

Mayaca is a lovely soft, small-leaved, light green plant. It's mossy in appearance and called bog moss locally where it grows naturally in southeastern North America. *Mayaca* also grows in Central and South America.

M. fluviatilis looks like a soft, fuzzy bush when grown in small groups. This is a nice plant that shows well in the tank but is difficult to grow. This plant needs high lighting, clean water, and usually additives, and doesn't do well if infested with algae.

Red foxtail can grow very fast under good conditions.

Micranthemum umbrosum

This is a popular, bright green plant most often used as a ground cover. *M. umbrosum* has small curled leaves with roots that grow along the stem and keep the plant at the bottom of the tank.

These are rather easy to plant; just try to get some of the stem in the ground, and in reasonable lighting, they should start growing soon and will look like they belong there in no time at all. Be sure to keep taller plants around your *M. umbrosum*

Don't get confused!!

There has been some confusion between *Micranthemum umbrosum* and *Hemianthus micranthemoides*. They are both small-leaved plants, but when you see them both, it becomes easy to tell the difference. *H. micranthemoides* like to grow upwards, except under intense lighting, where it may grow side shoots. Its leaves are small but flat and pointed, and it's a medium green color. *M. umbrosum* is a lighter green, and the leaves are more rounded and curl on the edges. It tends to grow along the gravel, with roots all along the stem.

trimmed so they don't block the light getting to the lower level of your tank and the plants you're trying to grow there.

M. umbrosum is one of the less difficult carpeting plants to grow. It's a very attractive and popular plant and should do well for you if you give it enough light.

Myriophyllum

M. heterophyllum, also called red foxtail or two-leaf water milfoil, is a native of the eastern United States. It has a lovely red color and nice leafage, similar to cabomba or hornwort. Red foxtail grows quickly and will tolerate moderate to high lighting, though it does better and shows more of the red coloring it's prized for in higher light levels.

Red foxtail does have a rather unusual growth pattern. The stems don't like to grow up straight but rather, tend to branch out a lot. This is nice in that the plant gets really full, but annoying when it takes over the whole tank. It almost doesn't matter how you plant this; it will probably grow no matter what. You could even just throw it in, and long roots will develop, reaching to the substrate. This plant will also need to be trimmed regularly.

A similar plant, *M. aquaticum*, is another one you may find at your local fish store or garden center. This is also called parrot's feather and is used quite a lot in ponds. Parrot's feather is bright green when grown submerged, but likes to grow across the top of the water, where it forms a different leaf shape. These plants aren't as happy in an aquarium as the red foxtail and will require more light.

Though parrot's feather is a native of South America, it has become established in different areas all over the world and is considered invasive. It isn't on the US Federal Noxious Weed List but is listed in some states and may be listed in other countries. You should check with local laws before working with *M. aquaticum*.

Najas guadalupensis

This plant is a North American native, though there are other species throughout the world. *N. guadalupensis* is a bushy green plant that has many branching stems with thin leaves. The stems are very fragile and break easily, each piece forming new plants. You can end up with these little guys all over your tanks, so this is another plant that will require upkeep, not only with trimming but with picking up the little pieces of plant around the tank. *N. guadalupensis* grows rapidly in moderate to high lighting. In higher light levels, the plant can take on some yellow and red tones.

The easy breakage of stems in the various *Najas* plants may make them a bit difficult in some planted tanks. You can plant them by trying to put them into the substrate lightly, though they often break when you do this. An easier method is to just set them on the substrate where you want them, put something else in front of them, and let them do their thing. They do tend to end up everywhere, so remove them regularly if you don't want a tank of just *Najas*. They are easy to remove and are no more trouble than trimming the fast-growing stemmed plants. This plant can also be a very effective in a breeding tank, especially when combined with a moss to cover the bottom.

Nesaea

These are plants from Africa, several of which occasionally become available to aquarists. They've been getting a lot of attention lately and have started to become more available. Several species have been offered for the aquarium, though *N. crassicaulis* seems to be the one most often available.

Nesaea are attractive plants but are difficult to grow and need good lighting to survive. The stems should be planted individually, or in very small groups, depending on the leaf size.

Potamogeton gayi

There are many *Potamogetons* throughout the world. *P. gayi* is a South American species that looks like a tall grass. Several other species of *Potamogeton* have a wider leaf, though they also grow on thin stems.

P. gayi will grow well in moderate to high light levels and is very hardy once established. A number of other attractive *Potamogeton* species are distributed worldwide. Some are more difficult to cultivate in an aquarium than others.

A few species of *Potamogeton* are available through various mail-order businesses. These plants have a tendency to ship poorly and often don't make the trip. If shipped in water,

> One of the most interesting things about these plants is that they grow not only from cuttings but also send out runners under the substrate, similar to Valisneria.

instead of the usual damp shipping, you'll have a better chance of getting your plants to your door alive.

Proserpinaca palustris

This native North American plant is also called mermaid's weed, and sometimes Australian *Hygrophila*. This is a slow-growing plant with attractive spiny leaves. It's not commonly found in the aquarium trade but is an interesting plant if you do find it.

The stems should be planted individually. *P. palustris* can also be grown emersed, though its leaf shape will change. This plant likes good lighting and grows very slowly.

Rotala

Three types of *Rotala* are most often available for the aquarium. Like the *Hygrophila*, the *Rotala* can grow in or out of the water, and their leaves will be quite different depending on where they are grown.

Rotala rotundifolia grows well under moderate to high lighting.

These are beautiful Asian plants that have a lot of red colors in the leaves when grown under the right conditions. Their coloring and interesting leaf shapes make them popular aquarium plants.

Rotala

Rotala rotundifolia produces flowers on terminal spikes (racemes) and differs from a previously introduced species, *Rotala indica*, which is an annual species with shorter, lateral flower spikes.

Rotala macrandra

This lovely Indian plant with bright red leaves makes a strong statement in the aquarium. It is difficult to grow, though, and requires strong lighting, good filtration, and nutritional additives to survive. The stems should be planted individually in clusters.

Rotala rotundifolia

Of the different types of *Rotala* available, *R. rotundifolia* is the most common and easiest to grow. There is some confusion between *R. rotundifolia* and *R. indica*. It appears that the most common currently held belief is that there is one plant, and that plant is *R. rotundifolia*.

R. rotundifolia will tolerate moderate light levels but does much better in higher light. It won't show pink on the leaves and stem in lower light, but in the higher light levels, both leaves and stem will attain a pink to red color.

You can plant a few stems together in bunches or whatever pattern you wish. They grow fast in good lighting and will need to be trimmed regularly. When reaching the top of the tank, *R. rotundifolia* can grow across the top of the water, forming a very densely foliated stem. Stems growing across the water will also often grow roots. You'll probably want to trim your plant before they do this.

Rotala wallichii

This is a lovely, fuzzy-looking red plant; it looks a lot like a red version of *Mayaca fluviatilis*. Like the *Mayaca*, *R. wallichii* is a difficult plant to grow.

Mexican oak leaves remain smaller under low-light conditions.

Zosterella dubia needs regular trimming to keep it from growing across the tank.

This plant requires a lot of lighting in a clean, well-filtered tank. It will also probably require added nutrients. *R. wallichii* does make a lovely focal point in the aquarium if you can get it to grow.

Shinnersia rivularis

Commonly called Mexican oak and also known as *Trichocoronis rivularis*, this is an interesting and attractive plant. Mexican oak can have a nice pink tint in higher light levels. Other colors have also been developed.

In lower light levels, the leaves will be more oval shaped, though some indentation of the leaves occurs near the water surface. For good indentation and more truly oak-shaped leaves, the plants need strong lighting. Stems should be planted individually in a large group.

Mexican oak likes to grow out of the water. The leaves grown emersed are a much more oak like, darker green. These plants tend to prefer to grow out of the tank and should be pruned regularly.

Zosterella dubia

This is an easy, fast-growing plant, and fun to say. *Z. dubia* is another plant that looks like a tall grass when kept trimmed. If left to grow, they like to cover the top of the tank. They can flower regularly when you allow them to grow across the water surface.

Z. dubia grows well in medium and high lighting. New plants can be started with cuttings. You can plant singly between other plants, which is how it will grow if left alone, or you can plant it in a bunch. If you do plant in a bunch, you'll need to regularly pull the plant, trim off the bottoms, and replant.

Rosette Plants

Many rosette plants can be grown in the aquarium, and some of the general favorites are these types of plants. The two largest families of aquarium plants are this type: the sword plants and the *Cryptocoyrne*.

The rosette plants grow from a central point in the plant. Both leaves and roots originate from that point. These plants have leaf stems but don't have the stems that the stemmed plants do.

Many large and beautiful rosette plants are often found in a central location in the aquarium. Rosette plants are also found in large patches of tall and short grass-like plants, and everywhere in between.

Sword plants are among the most popular and easily recognized groups of plants.

Planting and Trimming Rosette Plants

There are several ways to plant rosette plants depending on the plant and your preferences. The main idea is to get the plant roots under the substrate and keep the crown and leaves above it, without damaging the plant or making a big mess in your tank.

Before planting, check your rosette plant. It should be firm in the center, where the crown is. The roots grow out under the crown, and the stems with leaves grow out above it. Pinch off any leaves that are dying or have soft, mushy, or rotting stems. Be very careful not to damage the crown. It's okay if you leave a tiny bit of stem; it's better than taking off too much and hurting your plant.

If your rosette plant has a huge number of roots, you can trim some off to make it easier to plant. Many of the old roots will die and new ones will form anyway. Just be sure not to trim so much off that you have nothing left to hold the plant in the gravel, and be sure to stay away from those that are right next to the crown. The more leaves you have, the more roots you should leave.

When your plant is ready, you can decide which way you prefer to plant it. Some prefer to dig a space in the gravel and try to cover the roots. This can cause a mess, particularly if the tank is older and the gravel is filled with mulm and waste. You can also try making a hole in the gravel, slide the plant into it as deep as you can, then pull it back up to position the roots under the crown.

Another way to plant your rosette is to pull the plant into the place you want it from a small space away. The roots get pulled in under the gravel to the side of the plant, where you brought it into the substrate. This is how I prefer to plant, though if the plant is small enough, you only need to stick it straight into the gravel.

Propagation of Rosette Plants

There are two different ways that rosette plants propagate themselves: vegetatively and through seeds. They reproduce vegetatively through runners and side plants, and through seeds that can quickly grow into new plants.

Runners are the preferred means of reproduction for many of the grass-like plants such as *Vallisneria* and *Sagittaria*. They work very well, and these plants can quickly cover the floor of an aquarium they're happy in. Particularly with the taller varieties, these plants can take over an aquarium if not thinned regularly.

Cryptocoryne can also send out long side shoots that are a bit different from those of val and sag. *Cryptocoryne* send out a stem under the gravel that forms into a new plant.

Other rosette plants that will also form new plants around their bases include the popular sword plants,–the *Echinodorus*. Many sword plants also like to send up stems of blossoms that, after blooming, will start growing little plants. Some *Echinodorus* will produce a lot of plantlets this way.

Other plants, like *Aponogeton*, reproduce through seeds. Some can bloom and produce new plants in the aquarium.

Aponogeton

Aponogeton are plants that grow from bulbs. They're regularly found at aquarium stores and can even be purchased dry and dormant. The lovely Madagascar lace plants are part of this genus. In addition to Madagascar, these plants come from Africa and Asia.

Many of the *Aponogeton* are easy to grow, at least at first. These plants store energy in the bulbs and are all set to grow, but without nutrients, the plants will have trouble lasting, or coming back if they go dormant. Yes, go dormant–like tulips, daffodils, and onions, most *Aponogetons* are designed to live a cyclical life.

Fortunately, some plants are more hardy and can live several years before going dormant; these plants have been hybridized with other *Aponogeton*, and many of the plants now offered for sale can last quite a while if well cared for.

When plants go dormant, most should be removed. After removal, the bulbs can either be thrown away or they can be rested and you can attempt to resurrect them in the aquarium at a later date. The way you handle the bulb will depend on the species; most are kept moist and placed in other containers to rest in the refrigerator or another cool place before being placed back in the aquarium. Other species are best kept warm while resting. A few plants may be able to rest in the aquarium without removal and restart by themselves, but many will just rot.

If you look closely, you will see the leaves of a young Madagascar lace plant among the others.

A. rigidifolius is a bit different from the other Aponogetons. Instead of a bulb, it has a rhizome, like an iris plant, that several new plants can grow from. The rhizome can be cut and the new plants planted elsewhere.

The most commonly found *Aponogeton* in the aquarium trade often bloom easily. If you want to raise your chances for fertile seeds, brush the flowers daily with a cotton swab or similar item to transform pollen. Seeds will form on the stalk where the flowers were. These can be carefully planted to form new *Aponogeton* plants.

Many of the *Aponogeton* that are available for the aquarium trade are hybrids, and identification of the plants may be difficult. One that is usually easily recognizable and very desirable is the Madagascar lace plant. The leaves of this plant look like lacey skeletons, but can look somewhat different in shape depending on the original location and growing conditions. These can also be one of the more difficult to grow of the *Aponogeton*.

The most commonly found *Aponogeton* in the pet store is *A. crispus*, or a hybrid of it. Some other interesting *Aponogeton* that are sometimes available are *A. boivinianus*, with a dark-green crinkled leaf, and *A. undulatus*, with a medium-green wavy leaf.

Barclaya

A longtime favorite for its beauty and color, *B. longifolia* is a very desirable aquarium plant. It can be found in several color varieties that range from brown and red to green and hot pink.

B. longifolia can do very well or be difficult. It does have a reputation as a difficult plant, but it will often do well for a while. These plants tend to go into periods of dormancy that they may or may not recover from.

When this plant is happy, it can get very large. For long-term growth, it will probably need additional nutrients. *B. longifolia* grows from a rhizome, and if it's a large one, several areas may produce leaves. It is usually reproduced through seeds, and may flower and seed in the aquarium, sometimes producing new small plants.

Crinum

The *Crinum* has an onion-like bulb that sits on the gravel surface, and only the very bottom of the bulb and roots grow under the substrate. The *Crinum* genus has both aquatic and terrestrial plants, some of which are grown for the garden. These plants are also related to amaryllis.

There are several types of *Crinum* offered for aquarium use, and they are all fairly large plants. *C. thaianum* is common, and makes a nice alternative to jungle val, whose growth can get out of hand. Some of the other *Crinum* offered have more decorative leaves. These plants are easy to grow but will need a large tank.

Cryptocoryne

Crypts–not just for the dead!

Crypts are wonderful plants and are some of my favorites; they come in many shapes, sizes, and colors. Many *Cryptocorynes* are easy to grow and will even do well in moderate light levels. Though often considered somewhat slow-growing, in good lighting, they can form large clumps of plants in a surprisingly short amount of time.

Crypts do have flowers and create seeds, but they generally propagate in the aquarium vegetatively. Crypts produce runners, and new plants will form around older ones. Generally to start new plants, remove some of the plants in your clump and place them elsewhere. Some crypts may melt when being transplanted.

Xiphophorus nezahualcoyoti swim in front of crypts and other stemmed plants.

Cryptocoryne parva is tiny, but grows fast when established.

Even though crypts seem to grow slowly, they can eventually take over an aquarium.

Crypt meltdown

Crypt meltdown is something that just happens to these plants sometimes; though other plants can have melt-downs too, crypts seem to be the most likely to succumb. Often there is an underlying reason why these plants melt down. Usually they will only do so under extreme condi-tions, but sometimes, for some people, they seem to go for no apparent reason.

Just because your crypts have melteddowns doesn't mean they're dead. Often they will come back; just be sure to keep the area clean and remove any dead portions from the tank.

Many species of *Cryptocoryne* were originally found in Asia and New Guinea. Identification can be very difficult. Some species have different color varieties, and leaves of the same plants can look very different under dissimilar growing conditions, which can make it even harder to figure out exactly what you have.

A great crypt that is hard to find but interesting and low growing is *C. parva*. It's compact and stays extremely low. A bunch of them on your tank's bottom would look great!

One of the crypts most commonly found for the aquarium is *C. wendtii*. It comes in several colors. The leaves can look quite different depending on the conditions the plant is grown in, and they can grow into large clumps in a few months.

Another crypt to note is *C. ciliata*. This is a somewhat larger crypt with strong, bright green leaves. *C. ciliata* is one of the few plants that can not only tolerate, but even grow in brackish water. A number of plants can tolerate a small bit of salt, but *C. ciliata* will grow in water mixed with as much as 50 percent seawater.

Echinodorus

You won't likely get a cut from your sword plants. The term refers to the shape of the plants' leaves. These are popular aquarium plants from North and South America that are in the same family as the *Sagittaria* plants.

Sword plants are readily available in a variety of sizes, from the small pygmy chain sword to the larger melon swords. Many of the medium-sized swords are hybrids. These plants can be difficult to identify, and with the many varieties and hybrids available, deciding what you have can be a daunting task.

Some of the more commonly found swords go under the aforementioned names like pygmy chain sword, melon sword, and the ever-popular Amazon sword. Pygmy chain swords, *E. tenellus*, are fast-growing short plants that make nice ground covers. They're another one of my favorites and are a lot easier to grow than many other plants used for that purpose.

Amazon swords are medium to large plants. Often used for large central plants, they can grow under a wide range of lighting conditions. They do particularly well with filtered sunlight and appreciate peat moss or peat plates under the gravel, but can also grow without them. Swords can do very well without additives when grown by themselves or with other slow-growing plants. In a tank with mixed plants, they may have difficulty competing with faster-growing species and may need to be fertilized. Most swords sold under the name Amazon sword are *E. bleheri*, or more rarely, *E. amazonicus*.

C. ciliata can also be grown under brackish conditions.

The pygmy chain sword will quickly carpet an aquarium.

Other common swords are the large melon swords and the many color varieties they come in. These can be natural forms of the plants, cultivated forms, or hybrids. These plants are best in large tanks, and melon swords–especially the ones with color varieties–usually need more light than the Amazon swords.

Several other swords are sometimes available. Swords are usually easy to grow and are great plants for beginners. Many swords will bloom in your tank regularly, and often, small plantlets will form. These can be planted when they develop. Many swords will also produce additional plants that can be separated from the parent and planted elsewhere.

Eleocharis

Several hairgrass plants are sometimes offered for the aquarium. These plants, like their name implies, are very thin and grass-like. They can be kept short and grown in the front of the tank, or left long to grow elsewhere.

E. vivipara is the most likely to be found in the aquarium store. This plant is from North America; it's usually easy to grow and can be kept trimmed or left to grow tall.

Small plants will form on the ends of the blades; these can be left to eventually reach the top of the tank, or can be trimmed. The removed plants can be replanted to form more areas of growth. These are nice plants and form a good contrast to many of the other aquarium plants available.

Lilaeopsis

Often called micro sword, these plants can be planted to create a lovely effect in the aquarium, and can look very much

Amazon sword plants can bloom and develop little plants.

Many types of swords are available and most are quite colorful, too.

like the lawn in your front yard. These are highly valued plants to many aquarists, and can really look nice in your tank.

There are two species that are sometimes found for the aquarium: *L. brasiliensis* and *L. carolinensis*, which are from South and North America, respectively. *L. brasiliensis* is the most commonly found and is shorter than *L. carolinensis*.

Lilaeopsis are popular little plants but can be difficult to grow if they don't have the right conditions. These plants need strong light and added nutrients to grow well. They are often crowded out by many of the faster-growing ground covers.

A melon sword is shown here under filtered sunlight.

Nuphar, *Nymphaea*, and *Nymphoides*
Nuphar

These plants from North America, Europe, and Asia can occasionally become available for the aquarium. These plants can grow lovely emersed leaves, but they can also grow floating leaves and are very closely related to water lilies, which they can resemble at times, complete with attractive floating flowers.

The genus *Nuphar* has recently undergone some new classifications. For example, all North American *Nuphar*, such as the cape fear spadderdock, were previously classified as *N. lutea*, and they are now reclassified into eight different species. Names of these plants may be confusing for a while.

A small red sword plant is shown here with <u>Potamogeton</u>, hornwort, and a type of anacharis.

Part 6

Hairgrass grows behind a large patch of crypts.

These plants have rhizomes that are infamous for rotting easily. They can make beautiful aquarium plants if they're happy but can be difficult to grow.

Nymphaea

These lovely plants are usually found in the pond, but some water lilies can also be grown in the aquarium. Usually the floating leaves are removed to keep the plant growing emersed. The leaves that grow under the water can be very lovely. The large leaves are often interestingly spotted and come in colors from green to red. These plants need good lighting, and though they will often grow for a while, they need extra nutrients to grow in an aquarium long-term.

Nymphoides

Nymphoides aquatica is the unmistakable banana plant. These cute plants are easily recognizable by their interesting bunch of bananas. Most people don't realize these plants are actually a type of water lily. Roots grow out from between the bananas. Often, some of the leaves grow to the top of the aquarium and float. As with the other lily-type plants, pinching the leaves that grow to the top can encourage more lower leaf development. Occasionally, this plant will reproduce in the aquarium, but will do so freely in outside ponds.

Rorippa aquatica

Commonly called watercress, this plant may have several varieties. It can have very different-looking growth, and has the unusual quality of being able to produce small plants on its leaves. The variety called *Rorippa nasturtium-aquaticum* is a long-used spicy herb that is often used to flavor sandwiches and soups.

These plants are also suitable for the aquarium, though they can be slow growing. Some plants seem to tolerate low lighting, but do better in higher light levels.

Sagittaria

There are two genera of common grass-like aquarium plants, and *Sagittaria* is one of them. Some *Sagittaria* do have thin ribbon-like leaves, particularly those sold for the aquarium. Most species of *Sagittaria* grow large; and emersed; they are often used for ponds, but aren't suitable for the aquarium.

The species of *Sagittaria* used most in the aquarium is *S. subulata*. This species has several varieties of slightly differing heights and leaf widths. These plants are often sold under different species names. Regardless of the name the pet store gives your plants, they are nice plants and do well in the aquarium. *Sagittaria* are one of the older aquarium plants and have been used in tanks for many years.

Vallisneria can grow very tall and spread quickly.

Some *S. subulata* varieties will stay short, making lovely beds of grass in the foreground of your tank, and others will get taller and can be used in the back. They can tolerate a wide range of conditions, from soft to hard water and lower to high light levels. They will often bloom in the aquarium, sending small white flowers to the surface of the tank.

Samolus valerandi

These small, attractive plants are often available through pet stores, commonly sold under the name water primrose. They do look somewhat like the garden flower primrose in the structure of the plant and the shape of the leaves, but two are not related. *S. valerandi* grow emersed in nature, but with intense lighting, can be maintained in the aquarium.

Saururus cernuus

These plants, which are also called lizard's tail, grow emersed naturally but can grow well in the aquarium. They usually grow moderately slowly and stay small and attractive. Lizard's tails can also make nice group plantings.

Occasionally, these plants go through a huge and fast growth spurt. They can grow large leaves and a winding stem and look very much like a common philodendron houseplant. The plant can be trimmed back, and each segment with a node can be planted to form a new plant. At other times, you can cut or pinch off the end of the stem and replant to produce new plants.

Vallisneria

Vallisneria is a classic aquarium plant, with its lovely long ribbon-like growth. It's a fast-growing plant and can grow like a weed. The rapid growth characteristic is good for new setups, but it will quickly choke out other plants if it gets a chance. Without regular removal of new shoots, it can soon become the only plant in the tank.

Common Confusion

Vallisneria and *Sagittaria* are often similar in appearance and easily mistaken for one another. The tips of the leaves of the *Vallisneria* have little points that are called denticles. They are very small and may be difficult to see without a magnifying glass.

The *Vallisneria* can be rather confusing in regard to which one is which. Their growth can vary a great deal as well, which adds to the confusion. They all tend to like hard water, and can grow quite well if given the slightest chance.

Vallisneria will sometimes flower in the aquarium, producing small flowers at the top of the tank, but reproduction is through runners. These can be trimmed off and put in other areas of the aquarium or different tanks. Most of these plants look nicer in tall tanks. They can cover the tanks with their long leaves in shorter aquariums, but it's possible to trim the leaves shorter. Just cut them off with scissors at the desired length.

Ferns, Mosses, and Miscellaneous

Anubias

Anubias are attractive plants, with leaves that grow from a rhizome. They make lovely additions to the aquarium and can be suitable as a centerpiece plant. These are sometimes placed with rosette plants, but I put them in the miscellaneous category, as they don't really grow in a rosette pattern.

These plants are often variable in their appearance, even within the same species, and this has led to some confusion in their naming. About 20 years ago, they were recategorized into eight species. *A. barteri* has five varieties and several cultivated forms; it is the most commonly found *Anubias* in the aquarium

There are many other types of plants that can accent your aquatic garden.

hobby. The other seven *Anubias* species are *A. afzelii, A. gigantea, A. gilletii, A. gracilis, A. hastifolia, A. heterophylla,* and *A. pynaertii.*

Identifying the different *Anubias* can be a daunting task, but growing them is relatively easy. These lovely plants from Africa are related to a popular houseplant, the philodendron. The plants are not only similar in appearance, but like the philodendron, the *Anubias* are generally easy to keep alive. Sometimes they will even bloom in the aquarium.

The rhizome can grow along wood or rocks in the aquarium or be planted in the substrate. It can be tied to the item you want it to grow to with fishing line or cotton string. Be sure to tie it loosely, or else you may damage the plant. Many *Anubias* prefer moderate to lower lighting levels.

Ferns

Ferns are more primitive plants than those we've already looked at, though we did get a brief glance of ferns in the floating plants section. Their structure is more advanced than moss, but both sexually reproduce with spores. Frequently, ferns used in the aquarium reproduce using vegetative reproduction.

Bolbitis heudelotii

B. heudelotii is usually the only species found in pet stores. This lovely fern originates throughout Africa. *Bolbitis* is an interesting plant; the rhizome grows above the substrate, often tied to a rock or piece of wood. The dark green leaves grow from the rhizome.

This plant can be difficult and may grow better in soft, acid water. New plants are easily obtained from mature ones by clipping a leaved piece of the rhizome off the main plant.

The usefulness of Ceratopteris extends beyond the aquarium trade, as it is eaten in some cultures.

Ceratopteris

These attractive ferns can either float freely at the water surface or be planted in the substrate. *Ceratopteris* are found in aquatic and semiaquatic areas through most of the tropical and subtropical regions of the world. They are rather interesting plants in that young plants develop on the leaves of the adults.

These plants are also called water sprites or water ferns. It is often difficult to tell species apart, and there is debate in the scientific community as to the number of species. This plant lives naturally as an annual.

Water sprites are a longtime favorite plants among aquarists. They are useful as a top plant to hide fry and facilitate in the breeding of labyrinth fish. They can also be planted in the substrate and are an attractive aquarium plant. If they like the conditions of your aquarium, they can grow and spread very quickly.

Marsilea

This interesting fern can have quite a different growth form dependent on conditions. It's an old-time favorite and was often called four-leaf clover, because sometimes it does look very much like clover leaves on long stalks. But it also tends to grow in a two-leaf form and stays close to the ground. It seems very hardy and will grow in both high and lower light levels. It tends to grow taller, cloverlike leaves in lower light levels, and the two-leaf low-growing form in moderate to higher lighting, though this isn't always the case. I often will have both growth forms in the same tank, though mine tend to do the lower two-leaf form more often. There may be more than one species in the aquarium hobby.

Microsorum pteropus

Most commonly called Java fern, this is another longtime favorite plant among aquarists. These popular ferns can be easy to grow in various conditions. Java ferns can grow in strong to low lighting and will tolerate a wide range of hardness and pH, all qualities that have contributed to this plant's continued popularity.

Marsilea is a beautiful, low-growing fern.

Java ferns are popular and easy to grow.

Several attractive cultivars of this plant are often available. They can make a great addition to your aquarium.

When you plant your Java fern, treat it like *Bolbitis*. Java fern rhizomes should be anchored to wood or rocks rather than planted in the substrate. And once again, loosely tied fishing line or cotton string will work well to hold your fern until it has more firmly anchored itself.

Mosses

Mosses were probably the first terrestrial plants and are more primitive than the other plants kept in the aquarium.

There are three different types of mosses generally found in the aquarium. The first is an old standby, Java moss (*Vesicularia dubyana*); it is generally the thinnest of the mosses. The next is generally called fontinalis, shortened from *F. antipyretica*, and also sometimes called willow moss. It is more full than the Java moss, and its leaflike structures are spaced and have pointed ends. The third goes by Christmas tree moss and may also be a type of fontinalis. It's the bushiest of the mosses; the leaf structures often overlap and are fuller, with rounded ends.

Mosses look nice over gravel or on branches or rocks. Not only are they attractive, they're useful for breeding many types of fish. Mosses are also practical to use in bare tanks, since they don't have roots.

No matter which type of moss you grow, they are all very easy. Mosses will often grow under lower lighting conditions than most other aquarium plants. They also do well under higher lighting. Mosses can do so well that they can start to take over the whole tank if left unchecked. Luckily, it's easy to trim them or pull off the excess.

You can either let your moss grow over the bottom of the tank, where it will eventually start creeping over anything it can touch, or you can tie it to wood or rocks using fishing line or cotton thread.

Most mosses, like this Christmas tree moss, can grow up the sides of your aquarium.

Riccia

Riccia fluitans is an aquatic liverwort that has been popular in the aquarium for many years. This primitive plant was formerly used as a floating plant, which it does quite naturally in the aquarium.

Riccia has more recently been used to cover branches and rocks in the aquarium, a technique popularized by Takashi Amano in his *Nature Aquarium World* books. The *Riccia* is anchored to the branch or rock with fishing line or thread. After a while, the *Riccia* will grow to cover the thread and look like it grew there naturally. The effect is very attractive.

Algae

You might be thinking this is a misprint, but yes, people grow algae on purpose. One of the most interesting algae is the algae ball. These little green balls of algae are made in fast-moving water where the balls are turned regularly, creating the ball effect. They should also be turned in the aquarium regularly. Small pieces can be used to start new balls.

Other types of algae are also encouraged in the aquarium. Algae can give the aquarium a very natural look, as long as it's controlled and not a nasty tangle in the middle of your plants. Some of the hard, encrusting green algaes are often considered a sign of a healthy aquarium. I don't mind some algae in some of my tanks; it can look natural in the aquarium, because it is natural in nature. Beauty is in the eye of the beholder, so if you have pretty algae and you like it, don't worry about it.

Algae balls are just that, balls of algae.

Bladderworts

Usually if you have a bladderwort in your aquarium, it trailed in with another plant. If you've noticed it, you probably thought it was hair algae.

Bladderworts have thin branching segments with tiny leaves and bladders. These plants are like tiny Venus flytraps and catch tiny invertebrates.

Chara

This interesting plant looks a lot like the floating plant hornwort, but it's not a plant at all. Chara is a type of macroalgae and is also called stonewort or muskgrass. It has a strong garlicky smell when stem and leaflike parts of the algae are broken. It grows easily in the aquarium in both low and stronger light levels. It's not a typical aquarium plant, but it can be fun as an oddity.

Trees

Amazingly, you can even grow some trees in your aquarium. Many trees grow marginally along natural bodies of water.

One of the trees most often seen for the aquarium is the mangrove. These are usually grown as a part of reef aquariums, but they will also grow in brackish and fresh water.

Another tree that has been grown by some aquarists is the cypress. Both these trees would grow with the roots in the water and the top of the tree growing out above the water surface.

Organizations

Aquatic Gardeners Association (AGA)

AGA Membership

PO Box 51536

Denton, TX 76206

E-mail: membership@aquatic-gardeners.org

http://www.aquatic-gardeners.org/

American Killifish Association

Catherine Carney, Secretary

12723 Airport Road

Mt. Vernon, OH 43050

E-mail: schmidtcarney@ecr.net

www.aka.org

American Livebearer Association

Timothy Brady, Membership Chairman

5 Zerbe Street

Cressona, PA 17929-1513

Phone: (570) 385-0573

http://livebearers.org

Dallas – Ft. Worth Aquatic Plant Club

9846 Mixon Drive

Dallas, TX 75220

(214) 904-0704

http://www.aquatic-plants.org/

Federation of American Aquarium Societies (FAAS)

Secretary: Jane Benes

E-mail: Jbenes@yahoo.com

http://www.gcca.net/faas

Federation of British Aquatic Societies (FBAS)

Secretary: Vivienne Pearce

E-mail: Webmaster@fbas.co.uk

http://www.fbas.co.uk

Greater Washington Aquatic Plants Association (GWAPA)

22769 Portico Place

Brambleton, VA 20148

http://www.gwapa.org/

The International Federation of Online Clubs and Aquatic Societies (IFOCAS)

E-mail: ifocas@ifocas.fsworld.co.uk

http://www.ifocas.fsworld.co.uk

Publications

Tropical Fish Hobbyist Magazine

The Leading Aquarium Magazine For Over Half a Century

www.tfhmagazine.com

Tropical Fish Hobbyist Magazine has been the source of accurate, up-to-the minute, fascinating information on every facet of the aquarium hobby including freshwater fish, aquatic plants, marine aquaria, mini-reefs, and ponds for over 50 years. *TFH* will take you to new heights with its informative articles and stunning photos. With thousands of fish, plants, and other underwater creatures available, the hobbyist needs levelheaded advice about their care, maintenance, and breeding. *TFH* authors have the knowledge and experience to help make your aquarium sensational.

T.F.H. Publications, Inc.

1 TFH Plaza

3rd & Union Avenues

Neptune City, NJ 07753

Telephone: 1-888-859-9034

E-mail: info@tfh.com

Internet Resources

A World of Fish
www.aworldoffish.com

Aquaria Central
www.aquariacentral.com

Aqualink
www.aqualink.com

Aquarium Hobbyist
www.aquariumhobbyist.com

Cichlid Forum
www.cichlid-forum.com

Discus Page Holland
www.dph.nl

FINS: The Fish Information Service
http://fins.actwin.com

Fish Geeks
www.fishgeeks.com

Fish Index
www.fishindex.com

MyFishTank.Net
www.myfishtank.net

Planet Catfish
www.planetcatfish.com

Tropical Resources
www.tropicalresources.net

Wet Web Media
www.wetwebmedia.com

Books

Amano, Takashi
Nature Aquarium World, T.F.H. Publications, Inc., Neptune City, NJ, 1992.

Amano, Takashi
Nature Aquarium World: Book 2, T.F.H. Publications, Inc., Neptune City, NJ, 1994.

Amano, Takashi
Nature Aquariums World: Book 3, T.F.H. Publications, Inc., Neptune City, NJ, 1994.

Andrews, Dr. Chris
Hobbyist Guide to the Natural Aquarium, Tetra Press, Germany, 1991.

Axelrod, Glen S. and Brian M. Scott
Encyclopedia of Exotic Tropical Fishes for Freshwater Aquariums, T.F.H. Publications, Inc., Neptune City, NJ, 2005.

Binney, Ruth
The World Book Encyclopedia of Science, The Plant World, World Book Inc., Chicago, IL, 1985.

Innes, Dr. William T.
Exotic Aquarium Fishes 19th Edition, Metaframe Corporation, Division of Mattel, Inc., Maywood, NJ, 1966.

James, Barry
A Fishkeeper's Guide to Aquarium Plants, Salamander Books Ltd., London, United Kingdom, 1986.

Klee, Albert J.
The Toy Fish, A History of the Aquarium Hobby in American: The First One-Hundred Years, Revised Expanded Edition, Pascoag, Rhode Island, Finley Aquatic Books, 2003.

Margulis, Lynn and Karlene V. Schwartz
Five Kingdoms, An Illustrated Guide to the Phyla of Life on Earth, Third Edition, United States, W. H. Freeman and Company, 1998.

Rataj, Dr. Karel and Thomas J. Horeman
Aquarium Plants: Their Identification, Cultivation and Ecology, Neptune City, NJ, T.F.H. Publications, Inc., 1977.

Tepoot, Pablo
Aquarium Plants, The Practical Guide, New Life Publications, Homestead, Fl, 1998.

Windelov, Holger and Jiri Stodola
Holger Windelov's Tropical Color Catalog of Aquarium Plants, Neptune City, NJ, T.F.H. Publications, 1987.

Periodicals / Internet Articles

Anderson, Joe
Freshwater Shrimp in the Aquarium Description and General Information for the Interested Hobbyist,
http://www.thekrib.com/Fish/Shrimp/

Booth, George and Karla
Plant Pests,
http://aquaticconcepts.thekrib.com/Articles/Plant_Pests.htm, 2000

Cross, John W.
The Charms of Duckweed,
http://www.mobot.org/jwcross/duckweed/, 2002

Crowden, Dave
Shrimp Crabs and Crayfish, United Kingdom,
http://www.shrimpcrabsandcrayfish.co.uk/

Hennig, Matt,
Amano Versus Dutch-Two Art forms in Profile, TFH magazine, T.F.H. Publications, Inc., Neptune City, NJ, June 2003.
www.tfhmagazine.com

Naus, E.
Aquaworld, Netherlands,
http://aquaworld.netfirms.com/index.htm

Randall, Karen
The Aponogeton Family, The Krib
http://www.thekrib.com/Plants/Plants/apons-randall.html

Rook, Earl J. S.
A Boundary Waters Compendium, Aquatic Plants of the North,
http://www.rook.org/earl/bwca/nature/aquatics/index.html, 2002

Schoeler, Karl
In Search Of The African Cryptocoryne, http://www.mn-aquarium.org/masart12.htm

U.S. Army Corps of Engineers, Jacksonville District
Aquatic Plant Control Section, Salvinia molesta Possibly the World's Worst Weed,
http://www.saj.usace.army.mil/conops/apc/salvinia.pdf

U.S. Fish and Wildlife Service
North Carolina Noxious Weed Alert,
http://nc-es.fws.gov/act/noxweed.html

U.S. Geological Survey

Rotala rotundifolia,

http://www.fcsc.usgs.gov/Nonindigenous_Species/Rotala_r

otundifolia/rotala_rotundifolia.html

University of Florida

Center for Aquatic and Invasive Plants,

http://aquat1.ifas.ufl.edu/, 1995

Warne, Thomas R. and Leslie G. Hickok

C-Fern – A Plant for Teaching and Research,

http://cfern.bio.utk.edu/index.html, 1997-2002

Wilson, Rhonda

Natural Aquariums, Mesa, Arizona,

http://naturalaquariums.com, 1996-2004.

Index

Index to Scientific Names

Photo Credits

David Herlong, 70, 91

Horst Linke, 11, 17, 23, 31, 39, 42, 47-49, 55, 58-59, 61-62, 67, 71, 79-80, 87, 95-97, 101, 105, 116 (T&B)-117, 123, 141, 149, 155, 173, 185

M.P. & C. Piednoir, 64, 74, 83 (T&B), 92, 98, 113, 128

Marcus Russo, 124, 126-127

Ray Hunziker, 133

Rhonda Wilson, 13, 27, 82 (T&B), 88, 90, 92, 102-103 (T&B), 114-115, 120-121, 126, 129, 135, 142-144, 146-147 (T&B), 150-152, 158-160, 162-164, 166-167, 170-171 (T&B), 176-178 (T&B), 179 (T&B), 180 (T&B), 181 (T&B), 182-183, 187 (T), 188-189

T.F.H. Archives, 22, 76, 81, 118-119 (T&B), 153, 187 (B)

Takashi Amano, 19

Terry Anne Barber, 66, 69, 91 (T)

Cartoons by Michael Pifer

Illustrations by Terry Anne Barber